D0103605

Permission to Succeed

NOAH ST. JOHN

Health Communications, Inc.
Deerfield Beach, Florida

www.hci-online.com

Library of Congress Cataloging-in-Publication Data

St. John, Noah
    Permission to succeed / Noah St. John
        p.   cm.
    Includes bibliographical references.
    ISBN 1-55874-719-2
    1. Success—Psychological aspects.   I. Title.
BF637.S8S68   1999
158.1—dc21   99-22215
                                                       CIP

©1999 Noah St. John
ISBN 1-55874-719-2

Publisher: Health Communications, Inc.
            3201 S.W. 15th Street
            Deerfield Beach, Florida 33442-8190

Cover design by Lisa Camp
Book design by Lawna Patterson Oldfield

"This book made me understand, for the first time, why so many talented and creative people never achieve success—no matter how hard they try."

Gloria Michels
executive producer, American Television Productions

"Absolutely remarkable."

Paul Myers
editor, *TalkBiz News*

"Noah's concepts have been powerfully insightful, not only for me and building my business, but also for many of my patients."

Irene Mazer, Ph.D.
clinical psychologist

"Truly inspirational and powerfully insightful."

Vanessa Adams
career counselor

"This book is simply phenomenal! I have been reading success books for years and this is the first that simply explains why I and others like me do not let ourselves succeed—even though we already know HOW. It all finally makes sense. Superb!"

Paul A. Hughes
president, Gemini Video Productions

"Noah's techniques are so useful in dissolving deep-seated mental barriers to success that I have incorporated them into all of my courses. A 'must-read' for anyone who wants to be all that they can be."

Dr. Mark Koh
professor of change management, University of Malaysia

"I used to watch others succeed and wonder when it would be my turn. Thanks to this book, it's finally time!"

Judy Gilliland
president, Choice Enterprises

"What an eye-opener. I am on my third time through and am still discovering new things. I can't thank you enough, your book is more than worth the price."

Everette Burk
president, EGB Enterprises

"It's very simple: This book will change your life."

Clark Matthews
president, Louis & Clark Drugstores

"Finally, someone gets to the bottom of why people keep themselves from the success they desire. Noah does an outstanding job of naming the real cause of the 'fear of success,' and shows you how to overcome the problem once and for all!"

Cheryl Richardson
author, *Take Time for Your Life*

"I have read all of Noah's materials, and can honestly say, without exaggeration, that it has already had a profound effect on my life. Thank you so very much!"

Keith Andoos
sales manager

"I have worked through this book and delved deep for the answers to all the questions you ask in order to discern the lies about me that have paralyzed me all my life. With your help, I realized that I have many creative gifts and that I want to reawaken, to make my life larger and more fulfilling. I honestly can't tell you how much I appreciate you and your work. Thank you!"

Kyle Roberts
Alpine Industries

"Thank you for *Permission to Succeed*. It's a wonderful book. I've read it twice so far and can honestly say I don't think I've ever read anything quite like it. I am already applying the uplifting lessons learned and will refer to it often. And when my children are old enough, I hope to encourage them to learn the really very simple ways of successful living by finding your book among my most favorite classics of literature."

Brian Austin
Softwrite Services, Yorkshire, England

What People Are Saying About Permission to Succeed . . .

"Noah has created a remarkable system that transcends positive thinking and other motivational techniques to help you achieve success. Using a sense of humor and down-to-earth language, this book offers a step-by-step approach to help you create the life you want and deserve."

John Gray, Ph.D.
author, *Men Are from Mars, Women Are from Venus*

"Noah has achieved something remarkable with this book: He not only identifies what stops smart, creative people from achieving the level of success they're capable of, he also describes a practical, workable system to help you overcome these blocks. I highly recommend this book."

Joan Borysenko, Ph.D.
author, *Minding the Body, Mending the Mind*

"Noah's work represents one of the most significant breakthroughs in the study of success in years. If you want to eliminate the fear of success from your life forever, you owe it to yourself to buy this book."

Jack Canfield
coauthor, *Chicken Soup for the Soul* series

"What a great book! It can help anyone achieve their goals faster."

Roger Dawson
author, *Secrets of Power Negotiating*

"*Permission to Succeed* moves you from 'no-saying' into 'yes-being'! This splendid book is a beacon that will make you brighter and more sure-footed on your path to your life's purpose."

SARK
artist/author, *Succulent Wild Woman*

"This book is excellent. As I was reading it, I thought of a number of my friends who need to get it, because I *know* it will change their lives.

Audri Lanford, Ph.D.
former *Inc.* 500 CEO

"Transformative, powerful and practical. This information will change your life."

Ted Brandhurst, Ph.D.
research psychologist

"This book is a treasure for anyone who wants to be more successful. At last the answers!"

Dottie Walters
coauthor, *Speak and Grow Rich*

"This is a great book! I often deal with organizations who have success anorexia and the things you talk about are very useful for my personal success as well as my clients'."

Guy Sohie, Ph.D.
president, Global Insite

"My income increased more than 300 percent in just eighteen months as a direct result of using the principles described in this book."

Daniel Geist
Internet developer
Touchwood International

"Before reading this book, I wanted more success but had gotten used to not achieving it. Thank God for the day I discovered Noah's book! Now, my life is changing for the better, because the real ME is finally starting to prosper."

Robin Miller
president, RJM International, Inc.
South Africa

"I've followed Noah's simple step-by-step program and I'm already enjoying a new level of success, something I'd only dreamed about before. I'm amazed by how simple this process is and how quickly it works. I only wish this information had been available long ago."

Robert Chambers
president, Frontier Gold Corporation

CONTENTS

Part Four: Final Thoughts on Success

A LETTER TO THE READER

Dear Reader,

This book changes lives.

This book explains why you may feel more comfortable watching other people succeed rather than letting yourself succeed.

This book shows you why so many of us stop ourselves from succeeding and why no one could possibly stop our own success as adroitly as we do.

This book teaches you exactly why and how to stop starving yourself of the success you deserve in life.

This book will change your life—if you let it. Please . . . let it.

Warmly,
Noah St. John
Hadley, Massachusetts
August 1999

ACKNOWLEDGMENTS

The word *"acknowledge"* comes from an Old English word meaning "to recognize or to know." If there is one thing that I have finally recognized, it's that I can't do anything alone. At least not anything that is useful or valuable to anyone else.

We live in an interdependent universe. The idea of the "self-made man or woman" is simply false. For a long time, though, I believed that was what I should be. Through many trials and much error, I finally learned how mistaken I was. That being said, please allow me to thank the following people for their contributions to this book (whether they knew about it or not):

To my mentors in the self-help universe— Dale Carnegie, Dr. Napoleon Hill, Dr. Stephen Covey, Dr. John Gray, Neale Donald Walsch, Harvey Mackay and Dr. Richard Carlson— thank you for letting me know what is possible and for being there as my invisible counselors.

To Peggy Claude-Pierre, thank you from the bottom of my heart.

To Oprah Winfrey, thank you for bringing love, insight and compassion to a world that so desperately needs it.

To my two Judys, Judy Robinett and Judy Herrell, thank you for being there, for listening, for your patience, your intelligence and for your insights that I so deeply admire.

To Carol Helms, thank you for helping me get through a particularly difficult time in my life.

To all of my clients and students around the world, thank you.

To Dr. Bruce Coulombe, thank you for giving me my body back.

To William E. J. Doane, Neil Golden, Randy Wakerlin, Jamie O'Connell, Guy Harvey, David Bloomberg, Linda King, Clark Matthews, Steven Cournoyer, James Lowe and Dottie Walters, thank you for all of your love, support and encouragement.

To John Feudo, thank you for introducing me to Jack Canfield. To Jack Canfield, thank you for believing in my message enough to show my book to your publisher.

To Peter Vegso at HCI, thank you for seeing that this work will change people's lives, and for giving me the ability to reach many more people than I ever could have done alone.

To the entire HCI family, especially Teri Peluso,

Christine Belleris, Allison Janse, Kim Weiss, Maria Konicki, Randee Feldman, Kelly Maragni, Terry Burke and everyone on the marketing, production and sales teams, thank you for the strength of your vision and for all of your dedication and hard work on my behalf.

Thank you to Sheree Bykofsky, my wonderful, delightful, caring agent.

Thank you to my crack research staff: Elise Feeley of the Forbes Library in Northampton, Massachusetts. (Yes, she's the whole staff.)

Thank you to Hilary Stagg, whose CD *Dream Spiral* I must have listened to ten thousand times while producing this book. And to Wait Steinmetz of Steinmetz Photography for producing the best publicity shots of my career.

Finally, thank you to my mom, my dad, my brother, and my sister, without whom all the success in the world would be meaningless. Thank you for letting me know you're proud of me. I love you.

PART ONE

The Situation

1

A Winter's Tale

My breath steamed from my mouth and disappeared into the February evening. I had just become an ex-husband. Our divorce had not been bitter or hard-fought. We both knew it was for the best, and the entire courtroom procedure had taken less than ten minutes.

As I walked into the snow-covered night, a thought occurred to me. I had known exactly what I'd wanted in a wife. I had done what all of those self-help books and tapes had told me to do: made lists of the qualities I wanted in a wife; visualized the woman I wanted to be with; used affirmations—written and spoken words stating what my partner should be like. I'd even prayed to be brought to the right person. And even though my ex-wife and I had parted as friends, she was nothing like the person I had written, spoken or prayed about. Why had it happened? Why, I wondered, did I keep stopping myself from getting what I really wanted in life?

My breath stopped for a moment. I suddenly understood something that I had never understood before. I realized that my apparent lack of success had nothing to do with my not being smart enough, not driven enough, not talented enough or not persistent enough. I saw that something else was going on—something so subtle yet powerful, that it was preventing me from getting what I really wanted in life.

The next day, I called my father. I didn't really know what I was going to say to him.

"Dad?" I said.

"Yes?" he said. I took a deep breath.

"Is it okay with you if I succeed?"

There was a silence on the line.

"What?" he said.

"Well, I've been thinking. I've never been sure if it was okay for me to succeed. I've known that I wanted to be more successful than you, but I wasn't sure if that would be okay with you." I took another deep breath. "Would it be okay with you if I were more successful than you?"

There was another silence. Then my father did something I wasn't prepared for.

He laughed!

"Yes, Noah," he said. "I'm surprised you even need to ask me that. I thought you knew that your mother and I wanted you to be successful. I want you to be much more successful than I've been. Don't you know that's what we want for you?"

"Well, I just wasn't sure," I said. After another deep inhale I said, "So, it's really okay with you if I become more successful than you?" I wanted to be sure I had just heard what I thought I'd heard—what I desperately needed to hear.

"Yes, Noah. By all means. Please be much more successful than me."

I exhaled.

"Thanks, Dad," I said. "I needed that."

★ ★ ★

If you want to succeed, there is really only one thing you need. However, if you don't have this one thing, there is almost no way for you to succeed—or for you to enjoy success if it does come your way.

What is this one thing that you need to create and enjoy success—and what makes this book different from all the other self-help books out there?

You'll find the answers in the next chapter.

2

Why You Need Permission to Succeed

Have you ever gotten to the end of a self-help book and thought, "Was that it?"

Have you ever gone to a personal development seminar and said to yourself after it was over, "I already knew all that . . . so how come I'm still not doing what I know I'm capable of?"

Have you ever felt totally ready to make positive changes in your life, and then, a few days or weeks later, found yourself doing the same old thing, falling back into self-defeating habits and self-sabotaging patterns?

If so, you have more company than you might think.

Dan's Story

About a year ago, I saw a posting of an invitation to a teleconference about success. I remember being very annoyed about the timing. It was late in the evening and meant that I would have to stay in my office until around 10:00 P.M. and I wasn't looking forward to it. My voice of "reason" kept telling me that this was just going to be another one of those "Work harder and you will succeed" classes that I had been going to all my life. (I'd spent thousands of dollars on books, tapes, seminars and conferences, and none of them ever told me about anything that I wasn't already doing.)

This teleconference, though, was completely different. Finally, someone understood what I had been doing all my life. Please understand that outwardly, I was very "successful": I drove new cars, traveled, worked hard and made a good living. I had started a new job with an Internet marketing company that had really caught on fire. The only problem was that I couldn't really enjoy what was going on. I was being heaped with praise from co-workers and clients and my boss, but I didn't believe it . . . any of it. I would smile and thank people and then direct the praise to everyone else. I'd say things like, "Oh, thanks, but I couldn't have done it without so and so . . . he *really* did all the work, I just sold it." I didn't feel like I deserved any of the credit. I wouldn't allow myself the joy of succeeding.

In the teleconference, I heard some new ideas. Concepts such as "loving mirrors," "goal-free zones" and "giving myself permission to succeed." I felt as though someone had turned the lights on in a room where all there had been before was darkness. The room was beautiful! I was inspired . . . finally someone understood that I knew "what" to do, but that I had never given myself "permission" to do it.

Within about four months, as a direct result of using the techniques that Noah had described in his teleconference, I was promoted to sales manager with nearly a 30 percent raise in my base salary. My commissions went through the roof. Finally, I was successful . . . or so I thought.

But there was still a hole inside. Many things in my personal life were weighing me down. It seemed like the more successful I became professionally, the more miserable I became inside. I tried harder and harder to do all the "right things" so my life would be perfect. Talk about an impossible goal! I kept resisting the next step with Noah. I knew what I needed to do, but I would not do it because I still didn't feel like I deserved to be truly happy and successful.

Now I was in an even worse position. The lights were all on and I could see just how beautiful everything was, but I still didn't feel like I deserved any of it. I still hadn't given myself permission to succeed.

So I called Noah. He was very encouraging, but I kept lying to him that everything was fine and that I was well on the way to being successful. You know what's even sadder than lying to a friend about being successful? Lying to yourself about it. Noah knew I was not telling the truth, but he didn't make me feel bad about it. You see, at work I was still bringing in new clients and getting all kinds of praise, but inside, I felt less and less deserving of any of it. Old habits die hard, and I continued resisting.

Over the next few months, I went back to the old theories of "work harder" . . . "make more calls" . . . "go the extra mile" . . . but I just couldn't get success anorexia and giving myself permission to succeed out of my mind.

In October 1998, I arranged to meet with Noah at his office. We spent a great deal of time discussing how he discovered success anorexia and what he wanted to do to get the information to everyone who needed to hear about it. His conviction and excitement was contagious. I was again inspired, but this time I bought the book (the one that he had self-published and sold through his Web site).

After thanking Noah for his hospitality, I got back in my rental car for the drive back to New York and my flight home. I had the book in my possession and kept thinking about all the things Noah and I discussed. I made it to the airport and waited to board my plane. I was planning to read the book during the flight, but pulled it from my briefcase and read the introduction. Tears filled my eyes as I read. Having met Noah, I felt the words speak directly to my soul. It was overwhelming. I had to shut the book and put it away.

Less than one week later, I had been through the self-published version of *Permission to Succeed* at least four times. I now carry it in my briefcase wherever I go, in case I need to remember what's truly important in life. I called a friend two days after my visit with Noah. He said something that made me laugh and then he said, "Y'know, that's the first time I've ever heard you laugh." I was shocked. We tell each other jokes all the time and I distinctly remembered laughing at a joke he told me the week before. I pointed this out to him, and he replied, "No, you don't understand, that's the first time you've really sounded happy when you did it."

Thank you, Noah, for sticking with me and helping me to finally understand. My journey and my life have finally begun. . . .

★ ★ ★

I have a question for you. What do all of the following phrases have in common?

- Increase your sales
- Start your own business
- Lose weight
- Stop smoking
- Improve your self-esteem
- Raise healthy children
- Be more productive at work
- Have better relationships

The obvious answer is, they are important parts of many people's lives. However, what they also have in common is that they all describe effects that can be produced by doing certain things in a certain way.

For example, if you want to have better relationships, one thing you can do is to become a better listener. To help you do that, there are dozens of books, tapes and seminars that will teach you "how to become a better listener." The same goes for every one of the above phrases, along with hundreds of other subjects, ranging from "how to buy a house" to "how to build your own computer" to "how to raise ostriches."

The kind of self-help literature that I'm talking about is what I call "traditional success literature"—that is, the "how-to" information that you've been reading for years.

The purpose of traditional success literature is to teach you how to do something that you want to learn how to do. For example, when we put the words "how to" in front of the phrases listed above, we can see that the vast majority of self-help and personal-development literature covers what I call the "how to's of success." That is, it shows you how to do something that most people deem to be important in their personal or professional lives (e.g., "how to be a better manager," "how to lose weight," "how to get what you want in relationships," etc.).

At the risk of stepping on a few toes here, however, there is a question about traditional success literature that needs to be answered; and it is simply this:

If millions of people have studied traditional success literature for years, and they have truly dedicated themselves to the study of success—yet they still don't feel or are not successful—what does that tell us about traditional success literature?

There are three possible answers to this question. One possible conclusion is that people simply aren't trying hard enough to use the information they've been given. While this may indeed be the case with some people, it cannot be the case with all people who have tried to use this literature. In fact, the people I work with at The Success Clinic are among the hardest-working, most dedicated, intelligent, creative and committed people I've ever met. So I don't think that's the answer.

The second possibility is that traditional success literature is simply giving us the wrong information. Again, I don't think that's the case at all, because what's contained in most "how to succeed" books, tapes and seminars is actually very good material and can certainly help many people become more successful in life. (This is evidenced by the fact that it does work for many of the people who use it.)

What is it, then? If millions of people don't feel successful even after they've read and heard all the "how to succeed" information in the world—what does that tell us about traditional success literature?

The answer has nothing to do with either of the above factors: people not working hard enough or the information being wrong. The answer is that there is simply something missing from traditional success literature— and that without this missing piece, all of the hard work, good intentions and dedication in the world won't help a person succeed; and the best "how to" information on the planet will be rendered utterly useless.

What is this vital, essential piece of information that's been missing from traditional success literature all these years?

★ ★ ★

Before I answer that question, I'd like to share some words with you that were written by William James, who is often referred to as "the father of modern popular psychology." Near the beginning of the twentieth century, William James exploded onto the international stage by studying normal, healthy people and their responses to everyday life. He was the first person to take psychology out of the doctor's office and put it in the hands of regular people like you and me.

One of the most brilliant statements I've ever read about human beings came from the pen of William James. In *The Will to Believe and Other Essays in Popular Philosophy and Human Immortality*, he wrote: "One thing is clear: when we talk about human beings, we can see that they are not driven by logic or reason. Ultimately, human beings are driven by their emotions—by their *passional nature*."

In short, William James hit it right on the nose. We human beings are NOT run by the logical or reasonable part of ourselves; we are, in fact, run by what James called our *passional nature*—that part of us that isn't logical or rational; that is driven by emotions, desires and feelings; the part that feels pain, pleasure, ecstasy, anger, happiness, joy and loss.

Many people, particularly those of us raised in Western culture, tend to feel embarrassed or ashamed about the mere existence of our passional nature. Why? Perhaps because many of our Western societal institutions are built upon the premise that our passional nature is bad, wrong or immoral!

The question is, does it make sense to try and bury that part of us which makes us human? I'm not implying that we should run around like a bunch of crazed animals; I'm suggesting that many people refuse to even admit their passions exist (let alone that we are actually run by them), and that this refusal to accept or acknowledge who and what we really are has led to a lot of pain and unhappiness for more people than we can imagine. (The irony is that when we try to deny or bury our passional nature, we end up giving it more strength. We will explore this further in Part Two: The Condition.)

Our Passional Nature

What does our being run by our passional nature have to do with our success? Only everything.

You see, when I discovered the existence of a condition

that prevents smart, creative, talented people from allowing themselves to succeed (and you will see exactly how I discovered this condition, and what it means to you, in chapter 4), I realized that something simple—yet profound—had been missing from traditional success literature all these years.

It is simply this:

There exists a population of men and women—intelligent, creative, sensitive, caring, compassionate people—who are not succeeding NOT because they don't have the intelligence, skill, talent, education, drive or persistence to succeed . . .

. . . NOT because they don't want to succeed . . .

. . . NOT because they have a "fear of success" . . .

. . . NOT because they are "sabotaging themselves" . . .

. . . NOT because they don't try hard enough . . .

. . . NOT because they have to become more motivated . . .

. . . NOT even because they don't know HOW to succeed.

These individuals are not succeeding for only one reason:

They have never given themselves **permission to succeed.**

★ ★ ★

There is only one reason this book was written.

It isn't to teach you how to succeed, because you already know how to succeed.

It isn't to give you the latest tips, techniques or strategies of success, because you already know enough of them to be more successful than you can possibly imagine.

It isn't to motivate you, because you already have all the motivation you will ever need to get everything you've ever wanted.

It isn't to tell you to "think positively," because you've heard it a million times before yet you're still wondering why it doesn't seem to work the way it's advertised.

It isn't to get you to try something strange or weird, although you know that if you do the same thing over and over again, you'll get the same results.

The point is, you already know all of these things, and you don't need to hear them again from me.

No. This book was written for only one reason.

This book was written so that you will finally—once and for all—give yourself *permission to succeed*.

Why?

Because if you don't . . . you will never, and you can never, succeed.

★ ★ ★

If everybody wants to succeed, why do so many of us stop ourselves from getting the very thing we want most in life?

3

Why We Stop Ourselves from Success

Do you know people who have all the brains, talent and skill they need to succeed . . . but who are not achieving the success they are truly capable of?

Have you ever met somebody who finds it easy to start projects . . . but unbelievably difficult (if not impossible) to finish them?

Do you know people who keep getting close to success . . . but once they just about get there, sabotage themselves just short of reaching their goals?

Is it possible that you know someone like this intimately?

You are about to learn why so many of us do this. In Part Two: The Condition, you'll learn why these behaviors are actually created by a condition that I discovered (almost by accident), that eventually makes even the smartest, most talented people feel as though they can never achieve or enjoy their own success. In Part Three: The Solution, I'll show you how to remove the root causes of this condition, which will eliminate the behaviors that have stopped you from allowing yourself to succeed. Part Four: Final Thoughts on Success reveals why, even though so much has been written and spoken about this thing we call "success," it is still shrouded in an air of mystery, suspense and confusion; Part Four concludes with a definition of success that may very well change your life.

Ockham's Razor

Let's begin our journey by looking at why human beings do what we do. Have you ever noticed that there are enough theories about human behavior to practically drive you nuts? Have you also noticed that the more complex the theory is, the less it really helps you make positive changes in your life?

In scientific circles, there is actually a name for this phenomenon: it's called "Ockham's razor" after the fourteenth century philosopher William of Ockham. Ockham's razor simply means that the simpler an explanation is, the more likely it is to hold the truth. In this book, we are going to apply Ockham's razor to our study of human beings and human behavior. That means we won't be using complex psychological theories to explain human behavior; we're simply going to look at human behavior and ask ourselves, "Now why would they do that?"—and see if we can find the simplest answer to that question. Let's begin, then, with the most basic question we could ask about human behavior: "Why do human beings do what they do?"

Applying Ockham's razor, the simplest answer to this question is: *Human beings do something because it makes sense to them to do it.* In other words, people do things when they know why they should, can, want, need or would like to do it.

Now let's dig a little deeper. If human beings do something because it makes sense to them that they do it, then when human beings do something, they understand that they will derive a benefit from doing that thing or that some good will come from them doing that thing.

Look at an example. Why did you buy this book? Your answer to that question might be, "It has a cool title," "I liked the cover" or "A friend recommended it to me." However, these statements don't really tell the whole story. What were your reasons behind those reasons?

In other words, when you say, "I liked the title," what you're really saying is, "When I read the title, I believed that if I read this book, I would get something that I want more of (e.g., money, prestige, fame, success, etc.) and stop getting something that I want less of (e.g., failure, pain, lack of success, debt, etc.)." However, here's the essential question: Would you have bought (or even picked up) this book if there were not enough reasons compelling you to do so?

Of course, the answer is obvious: If you didn't have enough reasons compelling you to buy this book, then you would not have bought (or even looked at) it.

That part was easy. Now let's look at the flip side of this phenomenon.

What if I had shown or described to you all of the ways you could have bought this book? What if I told you that you could pay for this book with your Visa, MasterCard or American Express card, or with American dollars, Swiss francs, Russian rubles, Japanese yen or a herd of sheep?

What if I showed you that you could purchase it through a Web site, over the telephone, in person, at a retail store, through a catalog or from someone else who had already purchased it? What if I told you that you could find someone who already had this book, bop him on the head and take his copy while he's not looking?

Whether you would actually do any of these things or not, you must admit that these are all ways that you could have obtained this book (some weirder than others). Let's pretend, however, that I had shown you all of the ways you could obtain this book, but I had never bothered to tell you why you should buy this book, never mentioned what you would get from buying it. Would you have bought it then?

The answer, again, is obvious: of course not. But why not? Didn't I just tell you all of the ways you could get the book?

"Yes, Noah . . . but you didn't give me enough reasons to buy it."

Bingo!

Reasons Why Versus Ways How

Now, let's flip this illustration around again (because there are at least three sides to every story). Suppose you knew that you wanted this book. I mean you absolutely had to have it. Nothing, no power on Earth, was going to stop you from getting it. Would you have found a way to get this book?

You're darn right you would! If you had enough reasons compelling you to get this book, you would have done whatever it took to get a copy.

Have you ever seen people during the Christmas season fighting one another to get the "hot" toy of the season? Why are they acting like a bunch of idiots over a doll? They're acting that way because they honestly believe that they have to have that toy and have it *now*. That's why they're willing to do whatever it takes—bite, kick, stand in line for hours, act like hyenas—to get that toy.

What does this illustration show? (That human beings can be pretty silly, yes.) But what it really shows is that when human beings have enough reasons compelling them to do something, they will find a way (how) to do it.

You will notice that this aspect of human behavior has been addressed before in some traditional success literature. In fact, some of the best success literature ever written tells us "When you find a why, you will find a way." However, there is another side to this equation that has not been adequately addressed before, a factor so vital that it may be even more important to your success than finding "why" to do something.

This missing piece in traditional success literature is simply this: It's true that with enough reasons why to do something, a person will find a way to do it. (This is what I call the difference between the "why-to's" and the "how-to's" of success.)

But what about the "why-not-to's" of success?

Why-To's Versus Why-Not-To's

Remember, the purpose of traditional success literature is to teach you "how to" succeed. And since it's true that if you have enough "why-to's" (reasons) of getting or achieving something, you will find the "how-to's" (ways) to get it, some of the best works of traditional success literature have told you to focus on "why to" get something in order to find "how to" get it. That part makes sense, and it works—up to a point.

But let's say that you already know your "why-to's" of success. What about your "why-not-to's"?

What do I mean by your why-to's and your why-not-to's of success? Let me give you an example. What if I showed you something, and, for whatever reason, you decided that you really didn't want to do or get it. Think of something that you would never want to do. (When I do this exercise, I think of snorting cocaine, because I think it's the most disgusting thing in the world and something I would not permit myself or anyone I cared about to ever do). Can you think of something that you're really motivated to NOT do? (Kids: think "eat spinach.")

Now, when you think about this thing that you would never want to do, are you motivated to go out and do it? Of course not! We just said that you don't want to do it—and it's pretty clear that you're not motivated to do something you don't want to do, right?

I want you to think about the difference between not being motivated to do something, and being motivated to NOT do something. I'm splitting that infinitive for a reason. You see, there is a profound difference between not being motivated to do something, and being motivated to NOT do something. The former means we're just not doing anything to do or get the thing we're discussing. The latter means we are actively making sure that we don't do or get the thing we're talking about. In other words, we're not simply not moving towards it, we are actually moving directly away from it.

Why How-To's Are Not Enough

Now think of the thing that you really don't want again, the thing you're motivated to not get. What if I showed you all of the ways you could get it, this thing that you really don't want and that you're not comfortable with having in your life?

Using my example of snorting cocaine, what would happen if someone showed me how I could get some cocaine? What if they told me there was a special this week, and I could buy one bag and get one free? I'm using a ridiculous example to make a point: It really doesn't matter what someone said to me, I wouldn't buy or use cocaine for all the money in the world. This is because I have seen how drugs can destroy people, families and communities (plus I think it's just plain gross).

The point is that if you don't want something, or if you think that having, doing or getting something will bring you or those you love pain or unhappiness, you will be motivated to not get it—no matter what anyone else says about how to get it.

Remember our passional natures from chapter 2? If, at some emotional, gut (passional) level, we believe that getting that something means something bad for us or those around us, we will not get it—no matter what our logical or rational brains tell us.

Bottom line? If we have enough reasons why *not* to get something, we will not get it, no matter how many how-to's of getting it we know.

The Key Assumption That Traditional Success Literature Made— and Why It Ultimately Proved to Be False

Traditional success literature has helped millions of people (including me) to make better lives for themselves. That's because most of the "how-to-succeed" information that's been published in America is very useful and really does work. However, traditional success literature has also made a key assumption that ultimately proved to be false. This assumption was nearly invisible; it was so invisible that the people who wrote it didn't even realize it was there. In fact, until I "accidentally" discovered a condition that stops people from allowing themselves to succeed, no one had even been aware that this assumption was an assumption!

The assumption made in traditional success literature was simply this: You and I and everyone reading it had already given ourselves *permission to succeed*.

Why did this assumption take place? For a very simple reason. It was not done maliciously or with any ill intent on the part of the authors. It simply happened because the authors of traditional success literature never considered the possibility that anyone could NOT give themselves permission to succeed.

This was a very logical assumption to make; after all, the authors must have thought, quite reasonably, that anyone reading a "how-to-succeed" book would already know "why-to-succeed." However, what the authors of traditional success literature failed to take into account was just how powerful the "why-not-to's" of success really are, as we have just discussed (and will see more evidence of in part 2: The Condition).

Unfortunately, however, as we shall also see in part 2, what happened as a result of this assumption is that an astonishingly large number of people not only don't know they are allowed to succeed, millions of people actually believe that for them to even WANT to succeed is bad, wrong or immoral. They honestly (and unconsciously) believe that they can't or shouldn't or are not even allowed to succeed. This makes all of their efforts on the "how-to-succeed" plane of life less than useless, because they are quite literally pushing away the very thing they're trying so hard to "get."

Because the authors of traditional success literature assumed that we had already given ourselves permission to succeed (because it never occurred to them that we hadn't), they simply never mentioned to us what might happen to us if we didn't.

This single assumption has led millions of people to believe they were "the only one" with this problem; the only one who believes that it is bad or wrong for them to succeed; or that they were somehow "different" for believing that they were just not ever going to succeed, no matter how hard they tried.

★ ★ ★

That is why you are not reading a "how to succeed" book.

You are reading the first "why to let yourself succeed" book ever written.

★ ★ ★

What happens when an intelligent, sensitive, creative, compassionate human being—one who knows all about "how to succeed"—believes that he or she can't or shouldn't or is not allowed to succeed?

PART TWO

The Condition

4

How I Discovered
Success Anorexia

O n the morning of October 20, 1997, I
got up, meditated, showered, shaved
and ate breakfast as I had done
hundreds of times before. I was a thirty-year-
old college student only two semesters away
from earning my undergraduate degree in
comparative literature. I was also divorced,
living in a three-hundred-square-foot studio
apartment, and wondering when I would
figure out what to do with my life.

For about six months, I had been writing a
book about how leadership principles are
expressed through sacred literature. Well, the
truth is that I hadn't actually started the book

yet—I had been writing the *outline* for six months.

At the time, I felt as though I'd been studying success literature my entire life, yet I had practically nothing to show for it. My divorce had taken place exactly eight months before. I was on leave from my college studies (because I was trying to figure out what to do with my life), and I was resisting getting a job because I didn't want to spend time away from my book project. In other words, I was tired of working for other people at jobs I hated. However, since no one had offered to pay me for writing an outline for a book, I faced an uncertain financial future (another way of saying "I had no money").

I had no idea that by the end of the day, my life would change forever.

Earlier that week, I learned that a local college was going to host a free seminar about how to understand and treat eating disorders. I decided to go because: a) over the course of my life, I had met a lot of people who were anorexic or bulimic, and I thought the seminar might shed some light on the subject; and b) I really didn't have anything better to do. Plus, it was free.

Just before seven o'clock, I arrived at the seminar with about two hundred other people. The speaker was introduced and said that she was going to dispel many of the myths about what causes eating disorders, including: that the anorexic has been physically or sexually abused; that she or he is selfish, controlling or self-absorbed; or that she is trying to look like a model on TV. The speaker said that her experience with thousands of women and men who had nearly died from eating disorders showed that these individuals are actually:

- highly intelligent, very creative people
- overachievers (usually high-performing students or perfectionistic)
- intuitive and highly empathic—deeply in tune with other people's emotions
- caring, compassionate and concerned about other people's feelings
- hypersensitive to criticism or disapproval from others, particularly from their family members.

She said that these individuals also tend to believe that they are responsible for everyone else's feelings, are highly prone to depression and isolation, tend to withdraw from social situations, and usually suffer from intense self-loathing.

As she was speaking, I kept thinking to myself, "*Boy, this sounds just like me.*"

The speaker then said that she had discovered what really causes eating disorders: the fact that this intelligent, hypersensitive people become "of two minds." She called these the *Negative Mind* and the *Actual Mind*. She described the Negative Mind as an authoritative "voice" inside the individual's head that tells the anorexic such things as, "Everyone would be so much happier if you weren't around," "How could you be so selfish?", "You never do anything right," "Why don't you just die?"

Eventually, the speaker said, the individuals' Actual Mind (the speaker's term for the anorexic's real personality or actual self) becomes so weak from this constant barrage from the Negative Mind that they begin to believe that others would be happier if they simply weren't around. This causes anorexics to express their "lack of self" in such behaviors as self-inflicted pain, withdrawal from others and refusing to eat. Therefore, anorexics refuse to eat—not because they are trying to lose weight, but because they actually believe that life would be better if they weren't around.[1]

The Moment My Life Changed Forever

The speaker then said something that changed the course of my life. She said that eight times as many women as men develop eating disorders. The speaker also said that men who suffer from a deeply negative self-image probably express their "lack of self" in ways other

---

[1] *From a speech by Peggy Claude-Pierre at Mount Holyoke College, October 20, 1997.*

than an eating disorder. In the next few seconds, I had a totally unexpected realization—a moment of complete knowing; and in that moment, I knew that I had just discovered something that would change not only the course of my own life, but also the lives of people around the world. It was in that moment that the book you are holding was born.

In that moment, asked myself two simple questions: "Why do eight times as many women as men develop eating disorders? And why, if I identify so strongly with this description of someone with an eating disorder, did I not develop an eating disorder?"

I knew that it couldn't be because only women developed a deeply negative self-image; as I mentioned, I strongly identified with the description of someone with an eating disorder, and certainly identified with having a "lack of self." Therefore, I knew there had to be another explanation. But what was it?

In order to answer that question, I asked myself yet another question: "Is there a difference between where women have been told their worth lies, and where men have been told their worth lies?"

I instantly realized that there is indeed a significant difference between where women have been told their worth lies, and where men have been told their worth lies.

Where Women Have Been Told
Their Worth Lies

Let's back up a moment to see how I answered the questions I have just shared with you. Let me ask you: Where have women traditionally been told or taught their worth lies? Whenever I ask this question in my workshops and seminars, no matter where I am in the world, women will invariably answer: "In their bodies."

That is, women have been taught or told (literally, for centuries) that their worth lies in or is dependent upon their physical bodies (e.g. their looks or their outer appearance). Please notice what I am NOT saying. I am NOT saying that a woman's worth lies in her physical body. I am saying that this is what women have been *taught* or *told,* both implicitly and explicitly, in nearly every instance and in the vast majority of cases, for centuries. (Obviously, there are exceptions to this rule; however, based upon listening to the experiences of hundreds of women from Africa to Australia, it's clear that this experience holds true for the vast majority of the members of the female sex.)

Now, think about this for a moment. What would happen if someone who had been told or taught that her worth was dependent upon her physical body, were to develop a deeply negative self-belief, such that she began to believe that people would be happier if she were not around? Would it not make sense that that person would starve the very part of her that she felt held the most value—in other words, her physical body?

This was my reasoning at the seminar that night. That would explain why a person who develops a deeply negative self-belief would starve her physical body—because she would be attacking the part of herself that she (unconsciously) thought held the most value.

"Therefore," I reasoned, "in the case of a hypersensitive, intelligent person who developed a lack of self—and who had been taught that her worth lay in her physical body—the behavior that he would exhibit would be that she would refuse to eat (e.g. starve her physical body)." It was the simplest explanation I had ever heard of why an intelligent, sensitive person would starve herself of food.

Where Men Have Been Told Their Worth Lies

"What about men?" I continued. "Where have men been taught or told their worth lies?" It was clear that, whereas women have been told that their worth lies in their physical bodies, men have been told that their worth lies in their *material* body (e.g., their level of success, status, material possessions or position in society).

Again, please note that I am *not* saying that a man's worth lies in his level of success. I am saying that in the vast majority of cases, men have been *told* or *taught* that that is where their worth lies. (Again, this experience has been corroborated by men—and women, as well—everywhere I have taught on the planet.)

Therefore, I reasoned, "If a person who had been told that his worth was based on in his level of success developed a deeply negative self-belief, would it not make sense that he would starve the aspect of himself that he felt was the most valuable—in other words, his material body (as opposed to his physical body)?

"And wouldn't that mean," I continued, "that the outer, visible behavior exhibited by that person would be that they would *refuse to succeed?*"

Yes, I said to myself, *that does make sense*. In fact, that realization made more sense than anything I'd ever read or heard before on the subject of success.

At that moment, I realized that when a person's Negative Mind (which we will speak more about in the next chapter) produces a "lack of self" which manifests in their physical body, it creates "eating anorexia"—that is, the starvation of food. However, if that same mechanism (a deeply negative self-belief) were to cause a lack of self in a person who believes that their worth lies in their level of success, it would produce something that could only be called *the starvation of success*.

In that instant, I realized that I had just discovered something. It was a condition that millions of people were suffering from, but since no one had ever identified it before, it did not even have a name. I saw that I had just been given the responsibility to not just tell people that this condition existed but to give this condition a name.

The Condition with No Name

The fear of success. Self-sabotage. Have you ever wondered where these things come from or what creates them?

I had asked myself that question hundreds of times prior to that fateful seminar. On that night, however, I realized that I, like millions of others, had explained away my lack of success to "the fear of success" or "self-sabotage"—even though those had merely been empty phrases that offered no explanation as to why we do those things or how to stop doing them!

I had never heard anyone explain what actually creates the fear of success or self-sabotage as clearly as I had just seen. On that October night, I realized something that I had never heard or read in all my years of studying traditional success literature: that the fear of success and self-sabotage are not the causes of failure—rather, they are effects that are caused by something else.

For all of the above reasons and because of the realization that I have described to you, I—for whatever reason—suddenly became the first person to identify the existence of a condition that actually creates the fear of success and produces the behavior we normally call "self-sabotage." Since I discovered the condition, and had the responsibility to tell people about it, I realized that I had to come up with a name for it.

That's why I named this condition **success anorexia.**

What Is Success Anorexia?

Remember Ockham's razor—the understanding that the simplest explanation usually holds the most truth? Using Ockham's razor, we see that a simple truth has just unfolded itself before us; and it is this:

There are certain hypersensitive, intelligent, compassionate people who have developed a deeply negative self-belief. This often causes what can best be described as a "lack of self." When people with a deeply negative self-beliefs believe (because they have been taught) that their worth lies in their level of success (e.g., their material body), their lack of self can manifest as the starvation of success. That is, the outer, visible behavior exhibited by these people will be that they will refuse to succeed, just as someone with an eating disorder refuses to eat.

Therefore, these individuals suffer from what can most accurately be called success anorexia.

Now, I know it might sound weird or strange to some people, to talk about "refusing to succeed," "starving yourself of success" and success anorexia. But when we discover a new way of looking at something, we need to invent a new way of talking about it. Do we not speak of success in terms very similar to those we use for food? Who has not heard of "the sweet smell of success?" Or "the taste of victory, the fruits of our labors, our plans bearing fruit" and so on.

The point is, whether it sounds strange or not, this thing we call "success" is something humans hunger for—and, unfortunately, many of us are also starving ourselves of the very thing we want most. (The simplest definition that I have ever heard of what success really is, can be found in chapter 17.)

What About Women?

After reading the differences between where men and women have been taught their respective worth lies, you may be asking yourself, "Does that mean that women don't get success anorexia?"

Let's return again to Ockham's razor to answer this question. It seems clear that, whether it's politically correct to say or not (which it obviously isn't), women have traditionally been told that their worth or value lies in their physical bodies, whereas men have been told that their worth or value comes from their level of success.

However, it's also clear that women today work just as long and just as hard as men—often harder and longer!

Therefore, it seems likely that success anorexia would strike women today almost as much as it does men, because many women might now "buy" that their worth lies in their level of success (just as they've traditionally been taught that their worth lies in their physical bodies).

This is precisely the case. In fact, more than half of my clients and students are women.

Clearly, success anorexia affects men and women almost equally, nowhere near the 8 to 1 (women to men) ratio found in eating disorders. I believe that the reason for this nearly equal distribution of success anorexia between women and men simply reflects the growing presence of women in the workforce. It also means, however, that women are now not only starving themselves of food; they are also starving themselves of success. (Note: I believe that the main reason that more women than men contact me is that most men find it extremely difficult to reach out for help, whereas women are generally more encouraged to do so. See chapter 16.)

Again, please don't misunderstand what I'm saying. I am not saying that a woman's worth lies in her physical body or her appearance, or that a man's worth lies in his status or level of success. Any thinking person will realize that what I am saying is that these measurements are external ones society has placed upon both men and women, that bear no correlation whatsoever to any human being's actual, intrinsic worth or value.

Whether we like it, agree with it, or want to admit it or not, these external standards—appearance in women and success in men—have defined women's and men's status in society for centuries, perhaps as long as "society" itself has existed. I am neither defending nor supporting this fact, nor do I believe that this is the way it should be. I am simply stating a fact of the human condition.

If we dwell on these "politically correct" analyses, we're missing the entire point of this book. What's important to realize is that when an intelligent, compassionate, hypersensitive human being develops a deeply negative self-belief, what often occurs is either an eating disorder (e.g., the refusal to eat or the starvation of food) or a **success disorder**—the term I created to describe the refusal to succeed, or what I call the starvation of success.

Remember, the essence of my discovery is that what produces a success disorder is precisely the same mechanism that produces an eating disorder—that is, the temporary dominion of a person's deeply negative self-belief over his or her Authentic Self (a term we'll explore in more depth in the next chapter).

Are You Starving Yourself of Success?

Here is a very simple exercise that will help you understand this condition called success anorexia better. I'll bet that you may have kept a journal at one time in your life, or that you currently keep one. I would like to suggest that you start a journal as you go through this book, to help you overcome success anorexia. Throughout this book, I will refer to your journal as I recommend doing the simple exercises you will find at the end of some of the chapters. You may want to call this your "Allowing Success Journal." (By the way, I suggest that you choose a journal with a cover you like and the kind of paper you enjoy writing on. That way your writing will be a reward that you give yourself, rather than something you HAVE to do. Use a pen that you like, too.)

When you begin your Allowing Success Journal, I would like you to start with this simple exercise, because it will take you less than five minutes and will show you clearly where you stand in relation to this condition. All you need to do is complete the following sentences with the first thing that pops into your mind:

1. I believe that my worth lies in my . . .

2. I was taught that my worth comes from . . .

3. I believe that I have to . . .

4. I was told that I should . . .

5. My mother told me that I . . .

6. My father taught me that I . . .

7. I learned in school that I . . .

8. I should . . .

9. I have to . . .

10. If I'm good to myself, I . . .

11. If I say something nice about myself, I . . .

12. If someone says something nice to me, I . . .

13. When someone compliments me, I usually . . .

14. When someone is attracted to me, I . . .

15. When I'm happy, I . . .

There are no right or wrong answers; only *your* answers. The point of this exercise is to show you where you believe or have been taught your true worth lies— and to see if that belief is serving you or hurting you.

Whether you have a journal or not, please take five minutes and do the above exercise right now. By the way, did you know that the word *exercise* comes from a Latin word meaning "to unrestrain" (*ex-*, out of, *arcere*, to restrain)? Isn't that a neat way to look at the concept of "exercise"— instead of something that's a task to be avoided as long as possible, it is a way to *unrestrain* yourself?

When you are done with the above exercise, read your answers aloud to yourself. If you know someone who can listen to you without judgment, call them, explain what you are doing and read what you wrote out loud to that person. Ask them not to comment or to judge what you have written, but to simply listen. Did you know that all of these beliefs were in there? Did some of your answers surprise you?

Many, many people—far more than we can imagine, in fact—live every day being subjected to a deeply negative part of themselves; a part without pity or mercy; a part that seems bent on the person's own self-destruction.

★ ★ ★

Where does this negative self-belief come from—and what happens when sensitive, compassionate people become dominated by such a deeply negative part of themselves?

READER/CUSTOMER CARE SURVEY

We care about your opinions. Please take a moment to fill out this Reader Survey card and mail it back to us.
As a special **"thank you"** we'll send you exciting news about interesting books and a valuable **Gift Certificate**.

Please PRINT using ALL CAPS

Name

First [ ] M.I. [ ] Last Name [ ]

Address [ ]

City [ ] ST [ ] Zip [ ]

Phone # ([ ]) [ ] — [ ]   Fax # ([ ]) [ ] — [ ]

Email [ ]

(1) Gender:
___ Female   ___ Male

(2) Age:
___ 12 or under   ___ 40-59
___ 13-19   ___ 60+
___ 20-39

(3) Marital Status
___ Married
___ Single
___ Divorced/Widowed

(4) Did you receive this book as a gift?
___ Yes   ___ No

(5) How many Health Communications books have you bought or read?
___ 1   ___ 2-4   ___ 5+

(6) How did you find out about this book?
Please fill in ONE.
1) ___ Recommendation
2) ___ Store Display
3) ___ Bestseller List
4) ___ Online
5) ___ Advertisement
6) ___ Catalog/Mailing
7) ___ Interview/Review (TV, Radio, Print)

(7) Where do you usually buy books?
Please fill in your top TWO choices.
1) ___ Bookstore
2) ___ Religious Bookstore
3) ___ Online
4) ___ Book Club/Mail Order
5) ___ Price Club (Costco, Sam's Club, etc.)
6) ___ Retail Store (Target, Wal-Mart, etc.)

(9) What subjects do you enjoy reading about most? Rank only **FIVE**. Use 1 for your favorite, 2 for second favorite, etc.

	1	2	3	4	5
1) Parenting/Family	○	○	○	○	○
2) Relationships	○	○	○	○	○
3) Recovery/Addictions	○	○	○	○	○
4) Health/Nutrition	○	○	○	○	○
5) Christianity	○	○	○	○	○
6) Spirituality/Inspiration	○	○	○	○	○
7) Business Self-Help	○	○	○	○	○
8) Teen Issues	○	○	○	○	○
9) Sports	○	○	○	○	○

(14) What attracts you most to a book?
(Please rank 1-4 in order of preference.)

	1	2	3	4
1) Title	○	○	○	○
2) Cover Design	○	○	○	○
3) Author	○	○	○	○
4) Content	○	○	○	○

TAPE IN MIDDLE; DO NOT STAPLE

BUSINESS REPLY MAIL
FIRST-CLASS MAIL   PERMIT NO 45   DEERFIELD BEACH, FL

POSTAGE WILL BE PAID BY ADDRESSEE

HEALTH COMMUNICATIONS, INC.
3201 SW 15TH STREET
DEERFIELD BEACH FL 33442-9875

FOLD HERE

Comments:

5

What Causes Success Anorexia?

I'd like you to take a moment and do an exercise with me. (Since this is an imagination exercise, you won't even have to get out of your chair.) Imagine for a moment that you are standing in your bathroom, looking at yourself in the mirror. What do you see?

When you look at yourself in a bathroom mirror, the obvious answer is that you see a relatively accurate reflection of yourself (accurate, meaning two-dimensional).

Let's continue with this imagination exercise. What if, right next to your bathroom, there was a funhouse? You know, one of those places you go to at an amusement park with all kinds of goofy things designed to make you laugh (at yourself). Imagine that you are now walking into that funhouse and looking at yourself in a funhouse mirror. What do you see now?

When you look at yourself in a funhouse mirror, the obvious answer is that you see a distorted image of yourself—that is, an image or reflection that makes you look like something you are not.

For example, when you look in one of the funhouse mirrors, you might think you were seven feet tall, because that's what it makes you look like. When you look in another one, you might look two feet tall. The point is that when you see yourself in a funhouse mirror, you see a distorted reflection of yourself—one that does not accurately reflect the real you at all.

When you walked into the funhouse, did you actually become seven feet tall or two feet tall? Of course not. The reason that you look distorted is because the mirror you're looking into was designed to make you look that way; that is, someone designed the mirror to do that.

Is it the mirror's fault that you look like something you're not? No. Again, someone designed it to do that. Is it your fault that you believe what you see? No; it is not your fault either, because all you're doing is interpreting the images of light that you see. Therefore, no one is really "at fault" in this situation.

Okay, you already knew that your reflection in a funhouse mirror doesn't look like the real you and that your reflection in a bathroom mirror does. That's what they're both designed to do. But what if something really strange happened to you:

What if, for some reason, you forgot what you really looked like?

What if you had only ever seen yourself in a funhouse mirror? What if you had never seen what you actually look like (that is, accurately reflected in a bathroom mirror)? If this had happened to you, what would you be forced to believe about yourself?

If the only data your brain had received about yourself was inaccurate or distorted—that is, if you had only ever seen yourself in a funhouse mirror—you would have no choice but to believe that the image you saw in the funhouse mirror was what you really looked like. You would believe what you had seen.

This is what causes success anorexia.

What We Believe About Ourselves Is True for Us

The human organism has been designed so that we believe what our senses tell us is true.

Nature has designed us so that we accept as true the data we receive from our senses, until and unless we are given information that proves our senses to be inaccurate.

Therefore, if your senses (meaning your internal

senses) were saying things to you such as, "Everyone would be so much happier if I weren't around," and you had no other data (sensory input, such as another person) to tell you that this wasn't actually the case, you would have no choice but to believe that this message was true. And since our behavior comes from our beliefs, you would therefore act out those beliefs in the form of self-mutilating and self-abnegating behavior—simply because you were forced to believe a completely inaccurate picture of who you really are.

The Negative Reflection and Our Authentic Self

I use the above illustration to describe to my audiences why so many people suffer from such a deeply negative self-belief. To put it frankly, many of us were raised "in the funhouse." In other words, not only have many people never seen themselves as who they really are, they have absolutely no idea that the negative, distorted belief that they hold about themselves is not true.

I developed the term **Negative Reflection** to describe this phenomenon. The Negative Reflection is simply that part of us that doesn't believe anything good about us and instead only believes the worst.

The reason I use the term *Negative Reflection* is to help people see that this part of you is literally that: merely a reflection of your Authentic Self, or Who You Really Are (which we will discuss in a moment).

Where does our Negative Reflection come from? Some would say that we are born with it; others would say it develops because of the environment in which we were raised. I still prefer to use Ockham's razor, because I believe the simplest explanation is that it is a combination of both who we are (our basic personality, which we were born with) and our environment (the methods by which we were raised).

For example, any mother on earth will tell you that each one of her children had a distinct and very individual personality essentially from the time they arrived in this world. Contrary to what some "experts" say, we are not born as blank slates; we each are born with certain genetic characteristics and predispositions from the time we are born. For instance, something that would be terribly hurtful to one child might roll off another child's back with no ill effects whatsoever. Therefore, heredity and genetics—our basic, individual personality—play a significant role in determining whether or to what extent we develop a deeply negative self-belief.

However, it also seems obvious that environmental factors come into play as well in determining how dominant our Negative Reflection actually becomes. For example, if your parents or caregivers were emotionally distant, if you were constantly compared to other siblings or children outside your family, if you suffered physical, emotional or spiritual damage while growing up, these factors would obviously have a profound effect on producing feelings of shame, guilt and self-hatred later in life.

The point is in life, it is very rarely an either/or proposition. What we usually find is a both/and situation. The simplest way to describe the phenomenon of Negative Reflections is that certain people seem to be "wired" to develop them, while others simply aren't.

The next obvious question is: if the Negative Reflection is *not* who we really are, then what is?

Human beings have sought to answer this question since the dawn of recorded history. Humans have created scores of names for Who We Really Are: *soul, spirit, prana, chi, ki, atman, brahman, energy, the unknown knower, the unmoved mover* and so forth. The term that I use to describe Who We Really Are is simply our *Authentic Self*.

Whatever you choose to call it, it seems beyond doubt that something exists in each of us—the "still, small voice within"—that comprises the essence of Who We Really Are. I will talk more about this part of us in chapter 16; for now, let us say that it is the part of us that "knows beyond knowing."

The question is what happens when our Authentic Self begins to be dominated by our Negative Reflection?

The Bully in Your Head

When a bully comes up to you and demands your lunch money, you face a decision. If you stand up to the bully, he will either beat you up or he will back down. Eventually, if you keep standing up to the bully, he will get tired of your lack of submission and stop harassing you—because a bully's "strength" is not true strength at all, merely intimidation.

The Negative Reflection is like a bully in your head. It attacks our Authentic Self through intimidation and a constant barrage of self-negating inner messages. Ironically, and not surprisingly, our Negative Reflection knows what parts of us are weakest, and it attacks those weak parts of us with the most force, because that is precisely what a bully would do.

For example, Susan, one of my students, told me that she felt terribly guilty whenever she wanted something for herself, especially when she wanted to take a trip just for and by herself. She said that wanting to leave her family and work responsibilities made her feel incredibly guilty, and "selfish." Not surprisingly, she thought that being "selfish" meant that she was "bad." Therefore, this was a very effective message to stop her from doing the things she really wanted to do.

One of the things you will notice about the Negative Reflection is that it speaks in black or white, all or nothing terms: good/bad, right/wrong, always/never. It sees little if any room for the middle ground or an alternative solution. This, however, is one of the ways we face and actually overcome it, as we shall see in part 3: The Solution.

I began working with Susan by telling her that depriving herself in no way helped other people. I showed her that, in fact, depriving herself not only did NOT help others, it actually hurt those around her, because the people who loved her wanted her to have what made her happy. Also, we need to provide for ourselves so that we have energy to give others. While it was difficult for her to believe at first, she gradually realized that wanting to do things for herself in no way made her a bad person.

Susan's self-confidence began to increase, and in a matter of weeks, she was able to go to the mall and not feel guilty about buying something for herself. (This experience, by the way—feeling guilty about buying or doing things just for yourself—is much more common among my female students than my male students.)

Shortly thereafter, Susan finally was able to take her first vacation all by herself. She later told me that she had enjoyed not just going away, but all the steps leading up to the trip, because it was knowing that she could go—even more than the actual trip—that had made all the difference.

The point of this story is that the Negative Reflection is just that—a reflection of ourselves that is untrue. However, if we do not have any data or other people telling us that what this negative part of us says about ourselves is not true, we have no choice but to believe that it is, in fact, true. (This step—gaining positive sensory input from sources other than yourself—is the essential step to overcoming success anorexia, as we shall see beginning in chapter 9.)

For example, if you were raised in an environment where your faults or shortcomings were constantly and consistently brought up to you, where people did not appreciate or accept you for who you really are, it might be very difficult for you to know or to believe that Who You Really Are is good enough. You would be so used to hearing or believing that you're not good enough that when someone comes along and tells you that you are, you'd be highly disinclined to believe them.

In this manner, the Negative Reflection is reinforced by our fear-based society. With its survival-of-the-fittest mentality so prevalent, we are told to "do it to them before they do it to us." This is just one example of how the Negative Reflection manifests on a global scale. On a personal scale, however, it can simply take away people's ability to function or rob them of the belief that they have anything worthy to offer (see chapter 7 on Why We Dismiss Our Own Achievements).

The Dual Nature of the Human Being

This dual nature of the human being is most famously illustrated in *The Strange Case of Dr. Jekyll and Mr. Hyde*. Robert Louis Stevenson's tale of the mild-mannered Dr. Jekyll, who is transformed into the murderous Mr. Hyde (after drinking a potion that he himself created!), graphically depicts the two sides of human beings: our negative, destructive, "shadow" self and our compassionate, humane, true or authentic self.

An individual develops success anorexia because the Negative Reflection stops the person from asking for, reaching out for or accepting help from other people. The Negative Reflection knows that help from others spells its own demise. For this reason, victims of success disorders tend to isolate and withdraw from other people—not because they are antisocial, but because the Negative Reflection tells them that others just don't want them around.

One of the saddest ironies of this condition is that the very people who care most about helping others and humanity itself are the ones who are starving themselves of success the most, for the precise reason that they want to protect others from the "bad person" they think they are. In *The Strange Case of Dr. Jekyll and Mr. Hyde*, the story ends with the good doctor destroying himself to protect those around him from the murderous Mr. Hyde.

You do not have to protect anyone from yourself. More importantly, you must learn that the Negative Reflection is not at all Who You Really Are. In short, we must get you out of the funhouse . . . and back in front of a regular mirror.

How can we do that? You'll find the answers beginning in the next chapter.

6

The Seven Most Common Lies We Tell Ourselves and How to Overcome Them

Do any of the following phrases sound familiar to you?

1. You're never going to make it.

2. Nobody likes you.

3. Everyone would be happier if you weren't around.

4. If you want something for yourself, you're selfish; and since it's wrong to be selfish, you shouldn't want anything for yourself.

5. Since you didn't make your parents happy (or keep them together), you don't deserve to be happy, either.

6. If you were perfect, you'd get what you want, but since you're not perfect, you never will.

7. No matter how smart (clever, pretty, funny, charming, good, etc.) you think you are, you'll never succeed. Success is only for other people. Not you.

★ ★ ★

Every human being I've ever met has their own special blend of self-defeating inner messages they use against themselves. Some of my personal favorites are listed above. Here's what some of my students have said their Negative Reflection tells them on a daily basis:

• Why don't you just grow up?

• Stop being such a momma's boy!

• Why are you so stupid?

• Can't you do anything right?

• You're such a klutz.

• You're so fat, no one could ever love you.

• No one wants to be around you.

• People are only nice to you when you're there; they talk about you behind your back.

- You should be nice to everyone or else they won't like you.

- Why does everyone always leave you?

I'm sure each one of us has heard these messages at one time or another. The point is that some of us hear nothing but these messages all day long—even when we certainly don't deserve them. For example, Amy, one of my students, said that she was "met with blank stares" when she asked her friends why she felt so afraid of success. All Amy had done was start and direct a nonprofit cancer support foundation; write several books and numerous published articles about marketing and publicity; and travel from Missouri to Illinois to be with her mother as her mother was going through cancer treatment! To everyone else, Amy was the epitome of success, but inside, Amy felt like she was never doing or giving enough.

How to Deal with a Negative Reflection

As we discussed in chapter 5, the Negative Reflection, that part of ourselves that tells us "you're no good" is like a schoolyard bully. Yet when you simply face up to a bully you take away half of his power: the power to intimidate. A bully will frequently back down when someone stands up to him, because he's so used to everyone else backing down. I am simply suggesting that you stand up to this bully inside of your head and, by doing so, you will take away most of its power to intimidate you.

If you've spent nearly your whole life "in the funhouse" and have never seen yourself accurately reflected by those around you, it is likely that you literally don't know that this Negative Reflection is not Who You Really Are. If you believe, for example, that you are selfish, not good enough and unworthy of success (and whether someone told you these things in words or not is irrelevant) how can you be expected to act as if these statements are not true?

Each of these lies, and the Negative Reflection itself, gets its strength from only one source: your belief that they are true. However, if you've never been shown your real reflection, how are you supposed to know what you really look like?

What Would You Say to a Friend?

Let me ask you a question: What would you say to a friend who was starving herself of success? Would you say, "You're a loser, you can't do anything right; you don't even have a clue about how to live . . ."? Please! You would have a hard time saying these things to anybody, let alone to a friend. Why, then, if you couldn't say these things to anyone else, is it okay for you to say them to yourself?

The answer is that it is *not* okay for you to say these things to yourself. However, giving yourself these messages has simply become a habit. The good news is that habits can be broken. The most effective way to deal with a Negative Reflection, and therefore to change these habits of self-hatred and self-abnegation, is to treat it like the bully it is and stand up to it. Most of us try to hide when a bully starts intimidating us. Yet that's exactly what the bully wants us to do! Cowering and trying to hide only give it more strength. Instead of playing into its hands, stand up to your Negative Reflection by externalizing what it's saying to you, rather than hoping it will go away.

You can overcome your Negative Reflection when you realize that it's just like a vampire; it withers and dies in the light of day. The "light of day" means outside of your head, either on paper or being shared with another human being. Let's face it: Life can get pretty dark inside our own heads. When you get the Negative Reflection out of your head by writing it out or speaking aloud to another person, you immediately take away half—or more—of its power to control you.

A Simple Exercise That Demolishes Negative Thoughts

The Negative Reflection is also like Jack Nicholson's line from the movie *A Few Good Men*: "You can't handle the truth!" To get to "the truth," take a sheet of paper and draw a line down the middle of the paper. Write

"Negative Reflection" at the top of the left column, and "Authentic Self" at the top of the right column.

Take a deep breath. Now, without censoring or worrying about saying it right, write in the left column what you hear coming from your Negative Reflection. You may be astonished at how visceral and hateful the language of the Negative Reflection is. (That's why it's not called the "nice" reflection.) Remember, it has a job to do, which is to make you feel lousy. Amazing how well it does its job, isn't it?

Take as long as you want and get it all out there, so that you can see it on the paper in front of you. What you're doing is exposing the "vampire" to the light of day—which means its days are numbered.

When you have finished writing what you hear your Negative Reflection saying to you, pause. Take another deep breath. Now, write down what your Authentic Self is saying to you in the right column. "How will I know which voice is which?" I heard some of you ask. Good question!

Most Success Clinic students have reported to me that they can easily recognize the voice of the Negative Reflection, because they're so used to listening to it! Others have told me that it sounds like a disapproving parent or an unwelcome authority figure in their head. The easiest way to tell them apart is that the Negative Reflection won't have anything good to say about you. In fact, it would hardly be doing its job if it did. Remember, bullies aren't exactly known for their subtlety.

How, then, do you recognize your Authentic Self, if the only voice you've heard is that of the Negative Reflection? The answer is that you must first externalize the "bully" of the Negative Reflection, and then sit and listen patiently. Some people report that the voice of the Authentic Self is a quiet, certainly more peaceful, voice, one that has been literally "waiting" for them to notice it. Some say that it's more like a feeling than a voice—something sensed or known rather than spoken or heard. Many feel the voice as coming from their heart rather than their head (it's rare for the Negative Reflection to be located anywhere but the person's head). One person called her Authentic Self "the part of me I'd forgotten was even there, a part of me I thought had disappeared forever."

Here's an example of one person's experience with this exercise. Bill, a college student, wrote the following entries in his journal after learning this technique for externalizing the Negative Reflection and his Authentic Self:

Negative Reflection

You're not going to be able to write your papers because you are &^%$#/ up and know only how to fail. You are a betrayer. You have wasted your parents' money at college.

You are worthless, and more, you are a selfish $%&*/, good only at hurting people. Your friends deserve better than you can give. You should leave them so you don't have to betray them and hurt them anymore. You cannot accept responsibility for what you do, because you are afraid. You should be. Look at how much you've messed up before. You think you're special. How arrogant, how vain. You are no good. You aren't worth everything you've been given—talent, resources, money, friends, family, power—because someone else would have used it all a lot better by now. Everything you have done is pointless. Everything you try to do, you will eventually leave because you are a weak, directionless fool. You are a horrible human being. You should leave everything because you are not welcome or needed here. You are worthless. YOU LISTEN TO ME! YOU KNOW I'M RIGHT!

Authentic Self

Everything is different and requires an open mind to see. I will write my papers and need not worry about it, because I can do them. I can do anything. I know what's best for myself. My heart always shows me the next move. I am a loving, compassionate healer. I have been given talent, creativity, resources, friends, family and a great deal of power because I am going to need them for my life's work. I am worthy of my path. I can make no mistakes, for everything I do teaches me something new. I will fail, but that does not make me any less a person or any less amazing. I am allowed room to breathe and grow. It is vital to my health to get outside, to move when I would rather not take the first step of a long journey. Yet, if I don't, I am still a good person. I am on my own timing, not comparable to other people. I need other people to help back me up when I stumble, so a mole-hill doesn't become a mountain. I am inherently okay, because I am good. I am worthy of love, because I am a beautiful, amazing, human being. I am capable of loving, because I grow by sharing. I am truth. I know. Blessed be!

★ ★ ★

The Negative Reflection can only dominate its victims when it keeps them isolated and alone. When I tell my students that they're not losers, that we wouldn't be happier if they weren't here, and that other people really want and actually need them to succeed, it is as though they're hearing this information for the first time— which they usually are.

For example, a person with success anorexia believes that if she were perfect, then she would deserve success; but since she can never be perfect, she will never deserve success. She generally knows intellectually that she does not need to be perfect in order to be worthy of success, but we have already seen that we human beings are not run by our intellect, but by our passional natures (what we really believe).

We are not required to be perfect in order to deserve or enjoy success. One of the definitions of human is "prone to or characterized by the frailties and weaknesses

associated with humans as imperfect beings." Show me
the perfect person, and you'll be showing me no one. As
much as we would love to eliminate our faults and be
"perfect," it just ain't going to happen.

One of our main jobs as human beings is to accept that
we will never be perfect, yet we can continually strive to
improve ourselves. One of the great ironies of human life
is that we can never see ourselves as we truly are. We can
never appreciate or know our true value or worth to others, except as reflected through the eyes of others.

Remember the movie *It's a Wonderful Life*? Remember
how Jimmy Stewart's character, George Bailey, was about
to commit suicide because he thought he was a failure, and
that he would be better off dead? (A perfect example of
how the Negative Reflection shows us a completely distorted picture of reality!) Remember the final scene of the
movie. When people found out that George was in trouble, they poured out their hearts—and their wallets—to
him, because of all that he had done for them.

George Bailey was like all of us. He did not understand
that he had any value in life until Clarence the Angel
showed him what life would have been like without him.
Seeing how his presence, his one single life, touched so
many other lives made George want to live again!

It's the same for you and me. When you do the exercise
described above, you will see that you have been listening
to only one side, the negative side, of your mind. I am

not saying that you need to destroy or eliminate this part of you. It is neither possible nor necessary to do so in order to lead a happy life. Instead, what is required is a gradual turning from darkness into the light of truth— the truth that life needs you to be here, that you are here for a reason, and that none of us would be happier if you were not around.

These truths directly contradict what many of us have believed and been told for most of our lives. It is not necessary to eliminate darkness to enjoy the light. However, if we are to be and do what we are here to be and do, we must get the support we need to step out of the shadows of fear, self-hatred and loneliness. That is what the remainder of this book is about.

★ ★ ★

Please take five to ten minutes right now and do the simple exercise described in this chapter. Take out your Allowing Success Journal and draw a line down the middle of the page. Write "Negative Reflection" at the top of the left column, and "Authentic Self" at the top of the right column. Take a deep breath. Then write what you hear your Negative Reflection saying to you, and what your Authentic Self says in response.

You may be amazed at how viciously your Negative Reflection attacks you. Don't worry; it's just doing its job. You may also find that you have to listen closely and carefully to hear what your Authentic Self is saying to you. Please take the time right now to unrestrain yourself (remember that definition of "exercise"?) and write down what both parts of you have to say. I guarantee that if you do this exercise, you will discover many of the hidden reasons why you may be stopping yourself from gaining the success you want and deserve.

★ ★ ★

If so many people have been writing and thinking about success for so long, how is it possible that success anorexia has remained hidden for so long?

7

The Disguises
of Success Anorexia

So many words have been written and spoken about this thing we call "success" that it almost doesn't seem possible that no one discovered success anorexia before I did. However, let's look at some of what I call the "disguises" of success anorexia, to understand how and why this happened. (I'm going to present some of the more common manifestations of the condition in this chapter. In part 3: The Solution, you'll learn how to overcome these symptoms by eliminating what causes them in the first place.)

Life-Racing

First, we need to remember that someone suffering from success anorexia is being driven by the bully of their Negative Reflection, which constantly tells them things like, "You're such a burden to other people . . . You'll never make it . . . You're such a loser . . ." and so on. Most of the time, we aren't even consciously aware that these messages are going on inside; it just seems as if there's a constant "chatter" in our head that makes it quite difficult to feel good about ourselves.

This phenomenon has commonly been called "mind-racing": that is, the person's mind is constantly racing from one thought to another in order to avoid the painful thoughts that underlie the person's "busyness." What's important to understand in relation to success anorexia, however, is the effect that mind-racing produces in the person's life. My experience has shown that mind-racing produces the outer effect that I call *life-racing*.

Life-racing occurs when an individual, in an attempt to stave off painful feelings, keeps moving from one project to another, one job to another, even one area of the country to another. Often, when success appears close at hand, the person will suddenly move on to a completely different project, starting over at square one—because that's the only place he or she feels safe and comfortable.

For example, I once calculated how many times I had moved prior to my thirtieth birthday, and realized to my astonishment that I had moved thirty-eight times in thirty years—and the first fifteen of those had come before I was fifteen years old! As a result, I had become more comfortable moving than I was being in one place for an extended period of time (for example, a year). I distinctly remember going to a high school for the performing arts for my junior year of high school, and not being able to relax until I knew I wouldn't be back the following year.

The point is that it is not only excessively tiring to have to keep starting over from square one, doing that can never lead to success. This is certainly not a coincidence. I believe that a part of us knows that if we would just stick with one thing long enough, we would almost *have to* succeed.

Why We Dismiss Our Own Achievements

Another common disguise of success anorexia is to dismiss our own achievements, no matter how remarkable they are, as if they were nothing special, by using such statements to ourselves and others as, "It's no big deal. Anyone could have done it. Look at what I didn't do . . ."

Remember Amy, the woman who founded and ran a not-for-profit cancer research foundation while traveling from Michigan to Illinois, yet felt like she wasn't giving or doing enough? How about Dan, who constantly told the people who praised him, "I didn't do anything—I just sold it." Mark, another one of my students, told me that he had taught himself how to play the guitar, piano, bass and drums (and probably a few other instruments) before he was eighteen—yet he didn't think this was anything special!

The reason we feel very uncomfortable feeling good or allowing ourselves to be proud of our own achievements is simply because we believed our well-meaning parents or caregivers when they told us, "Don't get too big for your britches . . . Nobody likes a show-off . . . Don't be arrogant or people won't like you."

There is nothing wrong with not being arrogant. I am not suggesting that we go around telling everyone how great we are. Truly successful people do not need to tell everyone else how wonderful they think they are. Humility is indeed a virtue and a hallmark of a truly successful and happy person. Yet many of us have become *too* good at not believing that we are anything special— or even that we are good enough.

Because we so wanted to please our parents and make everyone happy, we (unconsciously) decided that the smartest way to do that was to make sure that everyone knew we didn't like ourselves that much. That way, when somebody criticized us, we could be sure that we would wallop ourselves ten times as hard. Have you ever noticed that no one else could possibly be as vicious to ourselves as we are?

The problem is that dismissing our own achievements has become a habit . . . then a self-fulfilling prophecy, for many people. Now some people can't even remember when they did anything that was good enough. Or they feel that they don't even have the merit to live.

The people whom I work with to help overcome success anorexia are, without question, the most intelligent, caring, talented and creative people I've ever met. The saddest part about doing what I do is seeing how little most people value themselves. Of course, it is the job of the Negative Reflection to make sure that we never feel good about ourselves or see anything good about ourselves. Unfortunately, it does a damn good job.

Lowlight Films

Another disguise of success anorexia is what I call *lowlight films*. I created this term when I realized that what we call "self-esteem" is really created by the images we continually play in our minds. For example, people with high self-esteem continually play messages in their minds that make them feel good about themselves. People with low self-esteem, on the other hand, continuously forget or overlook the good things they have done, and constantly remind themselves of the times they have "messed up" or fallen short of their goals.

Let me give you an example. Did you know that Michael Jordan, the greatest basketball player of all time, missed many more shots than he ever took; that he missed thirty-six shots at the end of a game that would have won the game for the Chicago Bulls; that for his first three seasons, the Bulls lost more games than they won; and that he suffered through seven heart-breaking ("character-building") seasons before he ever made it to the NBA Finals?

However (and this is why you and I and more than half of the people on the planet know who Michael Jordan is), once Michael got to the NBA Finals, he never lost one. He was named Most Valuable Player in every NBA Final in which he played. He won the scoring title in nearly every season he played in the NBA. And even though he missed many more shots than he ever made, oh, the ones he made!

When you see a film of Michael Jordan, what do you normally see? Do you see those first three losing seasons, those seven frustrating seasons before he made it to the NBA Finals—or do you see him slamming the ball home and kissing the championship trophy? Do you see all the shots he missed—or the incredible shots he made?

The answers are obvious: Of course you see the pictures of Michael Jordan triumphant, winning, successful.

That's why it's called a highlight film. Who would ever want to see a lowlight film?

However, have you ever noticed what most of us go around doing? Most of go around saying things to ourselves like: "If only I hadn't (messed something up) . . ." "If only I had (been given a break) . . ." "If only I hadn't (made that bad decision) . . ." "If only I had (known what to do) . . ."

Sound familiar? The point is we don't necessarily go around saying these things to ourselves in words, per se. (That is why most of us are not conscious of the messages we say to ourselves every day.) The human mind works in pictures and feelings. Therefore, what really happens is that those images of when we "messed up" or "lost" keep running and re-running in our minds, in what I call a "mind movie," until those negative images conjure up painful feelings that become permanently etched in our psyches.

When we project a picture onto the screen of our minds (e.g., a memory or mind movie), it creates a feeling, either positive or negative. This is exactly what happens when we see a movie in our outer life. For example, if you watch a movie of someone eating a lemon, it will produce the sensation of sourness in your mouth. When you read that sentence, didn't that happen, too? Didn't you taste the lemon in your mouth just as assuredly as if you had just bitten into it?

This is just an example of how powerful our minds really are. We have the ability to trick ourselves into believing something that hasn't even happened yet!

For example, one day when I was about six or seven, my father came home and was instructed by my mother to spank my brother and me because we had been "naughty." I don't remember what Josh and I had done, but I do know that whatever it was, it was Josh's idea. (The reason I know this is because he was older and always came up with the ideas. I just followed along like a good little brother.) My father, however, decided to start the spanking with me.

I remember being determined not to cry, because I did not want to give my father the satisfaction of "beating" me. This, of course, only made him spank me harder. When he finally finished, and it was time for my brother's spanking, my father turned to him and Josh immediately started crying, even though my father hadn't touched him yet.

"Why are you crying?" my father asked my older brother. "I haven't even hit you yet."

Josh was only about eight or nine. I have no idea how he thought of this, but at that moment he said, "Why wait until the last minute?"

Needless to say, my father laughed so hard that my brother never even got the spanking that I got!

Even though this is a funny story, I distinctly remember feeling that my father liked my brother more than he liked me. I remember deciding that if I were going to get along in my family, I had better become more like my older brother—and I tried desperately to do that, all the years I was growing up.

This is an example of what I call a lowlight film: a memory or mind movie that only serves to make us feel bad. The problem isn't that we make mistakes or that bad things happen to us; the problem is that we tend to keep replaying them over and over and over again in our minds—until we forget we've ever done anything right! Is it any wonder why so many people aren't very happy most of the time? (I discuss how to stop showing lowlight films in your mind in chapter 10.)

The Two Biggies: The Fear of Success and Self-Sabotage

Probably the most well-known symptoms of success anorexia are the so-called fear of success and self-sabotage. Let's examine these behaviors in the light of our new understanding of how the Negative Reflection manifests in the life of an intelligent, creative, sensitive individual.

Several years ago, social psychologists and other researchers began to examine the phenomenon of people who weren't so much afraid of failure as they were afraid of success. This went against much of the success literature that had been printed over the previous century, which had focused almost entirely upon helping people overcome the fear of failure. However, the "fear of success/self-sabotage" theory seemed to explain the behavior of many people who appeared to have all that was needed to succeed in life, yet who were not successful.

Research pointed to the existence of a fear that's produced when a person reaches a higher level of success than they're comfortable with, which causes them to fall back to a level where they feel more "comfortable" (even though the person doesn't really feel comfortable at all, and is constantly striving to find ways to improve their position). Since it was assumed that individuals in these cases were afraid of success, treatment for this behavior has focused upon overcoming individuals' fear of success—by showing them that success is nothing to be afraid of.

With the benefit of 20/20 hindsight, let's look at why, although this treatment does help some, it does not work for millions of people, and why there are so many people who still fear success more than they fear failure.

People with a success disorder are, by definition, highly intelligent, compassionate, creative and very sensitive to other people's needs. When people starve themselves of success, they are actually more sensitive to the needs of other people than they are to their own needs.

The success anorexic falls victim to the popularly held belief that says, "In order for one person to win, someone else has to lose." Examples of win/lose thinking can be found in every area of human life, including competitive sports, academia, business, politics and romantic relationships (where two or more people often compete for the same mate).

Most people do not realize that it's not only possible for us to win without taking away from others, but that a win for us can by definition mean a win for others. Let's look at an example.

Suppose you and I both want to build a hotel on a particular piece of land. There is only so much room on this parcel of land, so it's obvious that there can only be one hotel. You and I both put in bids on the land. We are in competition for what appears to be a scarce or limited resource.

If there is one word that sends shivers down the spines of success anorexics, it's the word *competition*, because that word implies just one thing to them: Someone must win, and someone must lose. Can you guess which role the success anorexic feels more comfortable (safe) in?

Why do certain people feel more comfortable losing than winning? Aren't we programmed from an early age that winning is the "American way"? We sure are, but what people who are sensitive to the needs of those less fortunate, to the environment and to the other creatures of the earth (not just human beings)? Wouldn't these persons see the devastation that human beings have produced upon the earth, and decide that when someone wins, it always seems to mean that someone else loses? Might not compassionate, sensitive individuals decide that winning brings with it too high of a price tag, and that the best way for them to win would be to make sure that they lose?

I'm not trying to be facetious or make it sound more complicated than it is. I'm trying to show that the Negative Reflection imprisons the success anorexic in a kind of twisted logic that says, "In order to win, you have to take away from someone else, and only bad people take from others. Since you want to win, you must be a bad person. Therefore, you shouldn't be allowed to win. Other people need it more than you do, anyway."

This tortuous logic causes success anorexics not just to be afraid of or to sabotage their own success, but to literally starve themselves of success in exactly the same way that nutritional anorexics starve themselves of food. Losing—not allowing yourself to win—becomes a habit that is next to impossible to break. As Vince Lombardi said, "Winning is a habit. Unfortunately, so is losing."

For example, Bobby, one of my students, told me that he used to play pool with his father. He knew he was a much better player than his father was, and Bobby's father knew it, too. Bobby would run the table until he got to the eight ball. He told me that he would invariably miss, scratch or "choke," and his father would win, when they both knew that Bobby deserved the victory.

Shortly after he learned to stop starving himself of success, Bobby called me.

"Guess what, Noah!" he said, nearly bursting with excitement. "I played pool with Bud [a friend] yesterday. I always used to scratch the eight ball with him, too. Guess what? I won three games in a row! I actually let myself win!"

"That's great," I said. "Did you have fun?"

"I sure did," he said.

"How did Bud take it?" I asked.

"After the third game," Bobby said, "he said, 'I'm tired. Let's do something else.'"

Although this incident may seem trivial, it's a perfect example of one of the hundreds of opportunities we're presented with every day. Whether we like it or want to admit it or not, much of human interaction consists of competition. When we're faced with a situation with a competitive element, a dialogue (usually beyond our level of conscious awareness) happens that goes something like this:

"What will happen if I win (beat this person or come out ahead)?"

"What if he gets upset/is jealous/doesn't like it?"

"What if she decides she doesn't like me/won't be my friend anymore?"

"What will my parents think?"

"Will people say I'm selfish for wanting what I
    want?"

"Maybe I should just let him win (again)."

I am not suggesting that every time people come
together that they compete for something. However,
we're fooling ourselves if we don't admit that one of the
prevalent components of life on earth is competition. If
you doubt the truth of that statement, just watch a
National Geographic wildlife documentary; human competition will seem pretty tame by comparison.

However, we can also remember that the word *competition* in its Latin root really means "to strive
together." We do not have to succumb to the belief that
says if one person wins, someone else has to lose. That
belief is simply not true anymore, particularly in today's
global economy.

Many business owners find that the best way to fail in
business is to not share information with their competi-
tors, because, with profit margins getting slimmer and
consumers getting smarter, the old tactics that used to
drive business such as keeping secrets and hoarding
information are not only obsolete, they practically guarantee failure today.

Let's return to the land and the hotel example. Instead
of going into a bidding war, perhaps you and I could

decide to do what's known as a joint venture, where you build the hotel and I build the restaurant that adjoins it. Or, I could build the hotel and you run a shuttle or limousine service that takes guests to and from the airport. Or a shopping mall. Or a petting zoo. Or a nature preserve. The possibilities are endless—but only when we see that one of the places a resource can be scarce is in our own minds.

Decisions, Decisions

Most people worry about decisions. We all want to make the right choices in life. But everyone has made decisions that, later on, made them wonder, "What was I thinking when that decision was made?" The key to remember about facing success anorexia, however, is that no choice ever feels right. Success anorexics tell themselves that if they made the decision, it must be a wrong decision. There doesn't seem to be any way out.

We each have to make several thousand choices every day. Many of these choices are mundane and quite trivial: "Should I put on my left or right sock first? Oatmeal or Wheaties? Butter or margarine?"—but many are relatively important: "Will I go to work today or stay home? Will I look for a job today or not? What kind of work do I really want to do? Who do I want to start a family with?"

Imagine having every decision you made, from the

clothes you chose to wear in the morning to what food you ate to who to marry to what kind of work you do, being run by a committee that always decided you were always wrong! Can you imagine how difficult it would be to just get through the day?

For example, I've been a great example of the phrase, "The human mind is a marvelous thing. It starts working the moment you are born and never stops until you meet someone you're attracted to." Whenever I met a woman I was attracted to, I focused so much on trying to impress her that I naturally turned into a blubbering idiot.

Gradually, I realized that my discomfort stemmed from that very thought that I had to impress her. Because I really didn't believe in myself very much, I tried to mask it behind a façade of false bravado. This strategy worked brilliantly and fooled everyone except everyone I ever met.

I also didn't realize that I was subjecting myself to a microscopic self-analysis that came from thoughts such as, "I hope I don't say something wrong. . . . I hope I don't make a mistake. . . . I bet she's looking at my nose." It's no wonder these women felt uncomfortable? And so did I!

What I didn't understand was that nearly everyone feels uncomfortable meeting someone new. When I realized that women were just as nervous and subjecting themselves to essentially the same self-analysis that I was, I relaxed. Then I realized that everyone is ten thousand times more interested in themselves than they are in me. People simply don't go home thinking about you or me; they go home thinking about themselves.

As soon as I realized this, I made one of the most important shifts in my thinking, the thought that has enabled me to rise above the voice of the Negative Reflection more than any other single thought: Since everyone is much more interested in themselves than in me, what if I became the one person who was just as interested in them as they are?

Instead of trying to be impressive, I made a decision to be impressed. Instead of trying to be fascinating, I made a decision to be fascinated. I switched from trying to be the center of attention to being the giver of attention. You can guess what happened. I finally began to (as the book said) "win friends and influence people," and my friends actually began calling me! That certainly hadn't been the case before, when I was so wrapped up in my little (negative) self that no one else could fit in.

It's important to remember that the fear of success/self-sabotage and all of the other symptoms of success anorexia are effects, not causes. These symptoms or effects are caused by the Negative Reflection's constant barrage of self-negating messages, which tells individuals that they must be perfect to deserve success, and since they're not making everyone else happy, they can't be perfect—so they're not allowed to succeed.

We must also remember that treating effects (symptoms) and not causes is like putting a bandage on someone who's having a heart attack. There is a deeper problem that cannot be solved by quick fixes, psyche-up motivation or positive thinking alone. Solving this deeper problem, and eliminating the causes of success anorexia, is what the remainder of this book is about.

★ ★ ★

Now that we know what success anorexia is, how do we overcome it?

PART THREE

The Solution

8

Why Overcome Success Anorexia?

The title of this chapter was originally "How to Overcome Success Anorexia." Then I realized that the title would mean I was focusing on the how-to's and making the same mistake that traditional success literature had made: assuming you already knew the why-to's!

Therefore, let me pose a question: Why do you think it's important to overcome success anorexia? Before you answer that question, let's look at what success anorexia does to people:

- Success anorexia makes people unable, incapable or unwilling to succeed. Examples of this effect appear throughout this book.

- Success anorexia makes people unable to enjoy success if they ever do succeed. Remember the person who would lose because he didn't feel comfortable winning?

- Success anorexia prevents intelligent people from using their intelligence, creative people from expressing their creativity, and sensitive people from using their sensitivity to help, serve, teach and inspire others, therefore robbing all of us of the enjoyment of their gifts, which humanity so desperately needs.

- Success anorexia causes the people who love and care about its victims to suffer. Every one of the people with this condition have family members and friends who love and care about them, who suffer when they do.

- Success anorexia drives people into debt, insolvency and bankruptcy. Money is an important measure of success in our society, although not necessarily the most important one. When someone starves himself of success, this self-abuse often emerges as a lack of money or material comfort.

- Success anorexia makes people take out their frustration, anger, self-loathing and self-hatred on themselves, which can lead to self-mutilation, loss of friendships and even suicide.

- Success anorexia causes people to remain unemployed or to work at jobs far beneath their intelligence or skill levels. Like money, our job or career is an important measure of our success—again, not necessarily the most important one. Success anorexia causes its victims to remain at a job where their skills and talents remain unused, unrecognized and unexpressed. (Just think of all the people you know who could be doing so much more with the gifts they've been given!)

- Success anorexia makes people wonder why they get up in the morning—or if they should even bother.

- Success anorexia makes people wonder why they should go on living—and not know how they can.

In short, success anorexia makes life a living hell for the people who suffer from it and causes those who care about its victims to suffer as well. After that analysis, isn't it clear that we should take immediate action to overcome success anorexia?

No. Not yet.

Even if you believe that all of the above reasons are serious and damaging enough to people's lives, one final aspect of success anorexia has been hinted at throughout this book and will now be clearly stated:

Life really wants you to succeed.

In fact, life desperately needs you to succeed.

If you really want to overcome success anorexia and stop starving yourself of the success you deserve, you need to believe this one statement above all others.

What on earth does this statement mean? Let's begin with the word *life*. What is life? Poets, philosophers, theologians and everyone else has been asking that question since we first looked up at the stars.

The simplest definition of life that I have found is that life is the actual environment or reality that exists in the universe. "Life" in this sense transcends human existence and includes all mineral, plant and animal life that can be found on earth.

Now that we've got that covered. . . .

The next phrase, "really wants," doesn't seem to make any sense. It is difficult for many of us to understand how life could want anything. Many of us were trained to believe that life is either something mysterious and unfathomable, or something that can be broken down into component parts and rearranged to fit the ideas of human beings. However, neither of these beliefs reflects the actual environment or reality that exists in the universe (remember, that's the definition of life that we're using).

Life is neither mysterious and unfathomable, nor can it be split into component parts that human beings want it to fit in. Life is, very simply, two things: love and law.

Love, in this sense, is the perfect unconditional love that exists between life and itself. There can be no separation between life and that which lives. Therefore, there is nothing for life to love other than itself. We humans are simply one form/expression/manifestation of life itself (rocks and trees and whales and every other form of life are other forms, expressions and manifestations of life itself).

Law is simply the set of principles that applies equally to the different forms of life, regardless of how that life is expressed, formed or manifested. An example of law is the principle of gravity, which is a natural law that affects all matter in the universe equally, without regard to who or what it is. No matter how nice, mean, tall, short, thin, fat, old or young you are, if you jump off a building, you're going to fall to the ground.

The Key to Life and Living: Why Positive Thinking Is Not Enough

The key to life and living is to understand that life can't break its own law. The first law of life is love: the perfect unconditional love that life has for itself. One way this expresses in our lives is that our thoughts are reflected back to us as our experiences.

"What do you mean?" you might say. "I've been thinking positively for years and I still don't have what I want. How is that an expression of love?"

Remember, you and I are much, much more than just our conscious thoughts. We are a complex system of thoughts, emotions, dreams, beliefs, values and principles, which are all subject to law. In fact, our conscious thoughts may make up less than 15 percent of all of our thought processes.

Let me give you an example. As I mentioned in chapter 4, I've been studying success literature since I was a boy. However, even though I diligently applied myself at whatever course or training program I studied, I eventually lost confidence and slid back into feelings of low self-esteem, because I never changed my underlying beliefs that told me, "Everyone would be so much happier if you weren't around."

You might say, where's the love in that example? Why didn't life support me? The answer is: Life did support me, but not in the way we've been trained to think it does. You see, after I studied traditional success literature—which, remember, is based mostly on how-to's—I worked diligently at the level of behavior, activity and motivation (all how-to's). For a time, I would be able to make small improvements in my life.

However, my underlying beliefs about why I couldn't or wasn't allowed to succeed hadn't changed. I still believed that it was better if others succeeded, not me. My Negative Reflection also kept telling me that if I became really successful, I would become a mean, selfish person (a great way to motivate me to stay away from success!).

Therefore, since I hadn't changed—indeed, was not even aware of—my underlying reasons for not succeeding, I could not permanently change my behaviors, attitudes or habits. I was diligently working at the level of how-to's, but I was not even aware of my why-to's or my why-not-to's. (Remember, when we work only at the level of how-to's, we're only using the tiniest portion of what truly motivates or allows us to do anything in life.)

The bottom line: Life perfectly reflected back to me—in the form of my experiences—my beliefs about myself and my relationship to other people. I believed that I shouldn't or was not allowed to succeed—and sure enough, I didn't let myself succeed! Life, therefore, supported my inner beliefs and what I "knew was right," regardless of what I said, how badly I wanted to succeed or what I did at the level of how-to's.

Was this unbelievably confusing? Incredibly frustrating? Enough to drive me to the brink of suicide?

Yes. It was.

Remember, trying to change your life through motivation or positive thinking alone is like driving east looking for a sunset. Your desire to see the sunset may be very strong; you may be an incredibly talented driver; you may be driving the most expensive car in the world; and you may be moving very fast toward your goal. But you'll never see the sunset as long as you're headed in the wrong direction.

If we're unconsciously stopping ourselves from success (because we inwardly believe that we can't, shouldn't or aren't allowed to succeed), we can think positively, write goals and work hard night and day . . . but we will never let ourselves succeed.

★ ★ ★

Rarely do we see life for what it really is. Our ideas about what life really is can't help but be shaped and distorted by the beliefs and experiences of our parents and grandparents, what we see on television and in the movies, and dozens of other, often contradictory and counterproductive forces. In addition, many of the people who try to tell us what life really is are called mystics, shamans, prophets, seers, gurus—or nuts.

We must be careful not to let our imaginations run away with us as we interpret life. Life simply is. Law simply is. Love simply is. Life is comprised of law and love. It really is that simple.

Here, then, is the answer to the question that opened this chapter, "Why is it important to overcome success anorexia?"

If you don't, life will be missing something very important.

You.

This awareness is deceptively simple. Chew on these ideas for a while. Reread this chapter and write your ideas about it in your journal. However, if you run too hard after these ideas, they may elude you.

After he had studied most of humanity's great philosophical, sacred and spiritual texts, the brilliant scholar Dr. Ernest Holmes created a teaching called The Science of Mind. Dr. Holmes's work has been the single greatest influence on my understanding of how and why the universe works the way it does. Dr. Holmes once wrote, "This thing called life is so simple, I find that I have to 'complex it up' to explain it to people."

★ ★ ★

Now that we know why to overcome success anorexia, what do we do first?

9

The First Step to Overcoming Success Anorexia: Unconditional Support and Loving Mirrors

Remember the exercise with the bathroom mirror and the funhouse mirror from chapter 5? Remember how the Negative Reflection is really a distorted image of the Authentic Self? Knowing what you now know about the Negative Reflection, what do you think would be the first step to overcoming success anorexia?

A Reality Check

The answer is "Get (back) in the bathroom." In other words, you need—perhaps for the first time—to see yourself as you really are, not as what you look like in the funhouse mirror. It's amazing and heartbreaking to see how many people have absolutely no idea that they have any worth or value outside of their job, their role in the family or what they achieve (awards, money or accolades). One of the great ironies of human life is that we can never see ourselves as we truly are but only as we are reflected through the eyes of others.

That means that we have the duty and the responsibility to become what I call **Loving Mirrors** to the people in our lives—particularly to ourselves. What is a Loving Mirror? Simply a person who can love you unconditionally. Someone who gives you the support you need. Someone who sees you as you really are.

This is the first and the only true job of the counselor, caregiver, parent, brother, sister or friend: to reflect love to people—to show them their Authentic Selves by loving and supporting them unconditionally. This is neither as easy nor as hard as it sounds.

You might want to take a moment and ask yourself these questions:

1. How many people in my life support me unconditionally?

2. How many love me for who I am, no matter what I do?

3. How many have ever seen past the façade that I put up, to the beauty and splendor that lies inside of me?

If you're like every other human being I've ever met, the number is not very large at all. If you're very lucky, the number is one or higher. Our job here on Earth is to learn, to grow and to contribute to life in some way—by expressing our gifts, talents and abilities. Part of learning is making mistakes. You've heard it before, and it's true: Nobody's perfect.

Success anorexics, however, because of a highly sensitive nature, have learned and believe a completely false and utterly debilitating contradiction: that they must be perfect in order to deserve to be happy or to succeed. Since they're not perfect, or even "good enough," however, they can't, shouldn't or are even allowed to succeed.

That's why their behavior is often called perfectionistic and controlling, and why they're often labeled overachievers and highly motivated. They really aren't trying to be perfect, as much as they honestly believe that they *have* to be perfect.

They are motivated not by a desire to improve themselves or to improve their station in life (a natural desire for any human being). Instead, they're motivated by a need to prove to the Negative Reflection bully that they are, in fact, worthy—which means trying to prove to this bully that they are perfect. The problem is that no matter how many perfect scores, awards or trophies they earn, the Negative Reflection never even comes close to being satisfied.

Let me give you an example. I once appeared on the game show *Concentration*. The show is comprised of a pictogram that is uncovered one square at a time. To uncover the puzzle, contestants have to match the prizes that appear under the squares. When you solve two puzzles in a row, you're eligible to try to win a new car.

I watched the show every day for six months prior to my appearance. Eventually, I knew the pictograms cold. I kept saying to myself, "All I want to do is win a trip to Hawaii or Australia."

I auditioned for the show when I arrived in Los Angeles and, sure enough, solved all the puzzles and passed their personality test (which proved that I had a personality). When I appeared on the show, I uncovered Wild Card after Wild Card, which meant that I could match up with any prize I wanted. Can you guess what trip they were giving away? You guessed it: a trip to Hawaii. Know what? I won it!

You'd think that I would be ecstatic, right? Guess again.

You see, after winning the trip to Hawaii, I won another game, which meant that I could try to win a new car. This contest was a race against the clock, where you had to match up seven different kinds of cars by uncovering boxes in under a minute. (This is a little tricky to explain in words.) I had a strategy all figured out. I would open up the boxes in a particular order that I had practiced for months.

Here I was on my favorite game show, the one I'd been dreaming about going on for six months. It unfolded exactly as I planned. I'd just won a trip to Hawaii. I was standing in front of these shiny new vehicles with the spokesmodels lounging on them. During a commercial break, one of the assistants on the show said to me, "You're going to win a car." I was beaming. We came back from the commercial. The clock started. I had forty-five seconds to match seven cars. Go!

I used the strategy I'd been practicing for months, and after thirty-five seconds had passed, I'd matched exactly . . . one car. I'd blown it, and I knew it.

Incredibly, I matched five of the remaining six cars in the next ten seconds. The last one, however, remained elusive and, alas, I did not win a new car. In the next match, I was up against a woman whom I had met back-stage. I felt mighty smug, thinking that I knew I could beat her. However, I also had a funny feeling in my gut, a feeling that I was not going to win. My feeling proved right. She beat me by a wide margin . . . then proceeded to win a new truck!

When I got home, I felt exhausted, beaten and lousy. I called my parents, whom I wanted to surprise with the news that I'd been on my favorite game show. I told them I'd just won a trip to Hawaii. Was I ecstatic? Was I psyched?

No. I was bummed—all because I didn't win a new car. I felt like I'd failed.

Never mind that I had made it on to my favorite game show, that all of those months of hard work and study had finally paid off. Never mind that I had just won a trip to Hawaii—literally my dream vacation—and that I was going to fly there free and be given $350 in spending money to boot. Never mind that I had just met Alex Trebek and had a blast on national television. No, I was bummed because all I could see was what I *didn't* do, where I had failed and come up short. All because I didn't win a new car (one that, at the time, I couldn't have afforded to pay the taxes on anyway).

Amazing what the Negative Reflection can make us do to ourselves, isn't it?

★ ★ ★

As with anything, the place we must start is at the beginning.

Many people in our culture have been raised in an environment where love is given very conditionally. That means, if you did the right things, if you performed or conformed, if you showed up in the ways that your parents or elders wanted, you were given "love." However, if, for whatever reason, you did not show up in the right ways or do the right things, most parents or elders withdrew their love, thereby punishing you and serving as a deterrent to incorrect behavior.

All human beings need to be loved unconditionally in order to express the best of themselves and believe in themselves. When children, particularly hypersensitive ones, feel that love is given conditionally, those children are forced to believe that they only deserve love (e.g., are good enough or worthy of love) when and if they perform or conform.

What does conditional love really mean? How is it different from unconditional love—and why is unconditional love the key to overcoming success anorexia? Let's start with what conditional love looks like. Conditional love goes something like this: "If you show up the way I expect you to, if you do the things I expect of you and do what I say, if you perform for me and for other people the way you're supposed to, then I will love you." Sound familiar to anyone?

If that's conditional love, it's pretty easy to see that unconditional love is simply the opposite. Unconditional love goes something like this: "I love you no matter what you do and no matter who you are. Whether you perform, get perfect grades or show up for me in the ways that I want or expect you to do, I'm going to love you anyway."

Some of you may be thinking, "Come on, Noah, isn't that a pretty permissive attitude? Are you saying that we should just let people do whatever they want?"

Not at all. I am not saying that we should become permissive and just let everyone do anything they want to do. Let me give you an example. I recently attended one of the nation's most distinctive liberal arts colleges to get my bachelor's degree. (This was my second time in college, after spending a decade in the world of business, which gave me the distinct advantage of being ten years older than most of my classmates!)

During my time there, I noticed something fascinating (and rather unnerving) about many of my classmates. They had been raised by "children of the sixties," which meant that their parents had become adults in a time of defiance and rebellion, when many rules of social behavior and conformity were thrown out the window.

I noticed that many of my classmates seemed to have been raised in an environment whose philosophy could essentially be boiled down to one word: "Whatever." Meaning, "Whatever you do is okay with me."

Now, this may sound good at first glance; after all, what child likes to be punished or be given rules to live by? However, there is a problem with this line of thinking: When children are raised without boundaries or guidelines, when they learn that anything they do is okay, they learn that there are no consequences to their actions. That means these children grow into adults who believe that "I can do whatever I want and that's okay."

Let's take this belief to its logical end. If I had been raised like this, I would believe something like this: If I want to take something from someone else, I can just go into their house and take it, right? What if I wanted to sell drugs? No problem, right? How about hurting or killing innocent people?

Do you see the problem here? The problem is, while we might not like everything about the society in which we live, society exists for a reason. Human society evolved in order for human beings to exist both individually and as a group. We may complain that "society" puts unfair demands on us, and perhaps that's true. Yet the fact remains that without this thing we call "society," most of us would not be able to survive for very long.

The point is that there are consequences to our actions, although we may not see the consequences of the actions we take today for weeks, months, or even years or decades. (The word "consequence" literally means "to follow closely.")

Therefore, when we talk about unconditional love, it's also important to know what we're not talking about. We're not talking about letting people do whatever the hell they want! We're not talking about permissiveness. We're not talking about letting people walk all over us and say whatever they feel like saying. What we're talking about is precisely the opposite of those things.

Notice again what unconditional love is. Unconditional love says, "I'm going to love you no matter what." It does NOT say, "Anything you do is okay." Let me ask you: Would it be okay with you if your child stole something from one of your neighbors? Would it be okay with you if your boss or your employee embezzled from your company? Would it be okay with you if your customers or your suppliers ripped you off? It darn well shouldn't be.

If those things aren't okay, what is? Where do we start? Again, we have to start at the beginning. There is a profound difference between saying "I'm going to love you no matter what" and "Anything you do is okay" (meaning, you can do whatever you want and there won't be any consequences to your actions). Do you see the difference?

People who were raised with the message "Anything you do is okay" actually have a very difficult time in life, because this is so utterly incorrect and not the way life really operates. People who act this way typically find themselves shut out of society and wonder why.

However, can you see how people who get the other message from their parents or elders, "I'm going to love you no matter what," are literally given the strength to move mountains?

Here's a good example. When Tiger Woods, as a second grader, entered his first golf competition—an international competition for young golfers—tension hung in the air. The young boys wanted to do well to please their parents and the crowd of onlookers. Just as the competition was about to get underway, Tiger's father went up to Tiger and said, "Son, I want you to know that I love you no matter how you do. Enjoy yourself."

Tiger walked up to the first tee, blasted his ball down the middle of the fairway, and went on to win the tournament. After the tournament was over, his father asked him what he was thinking about as he stood over that first shot. Tiger looked up at his father and said, "Where I wanted my ball to go, Daddy."[1]

How many of the other boys do you think were able to concentrate on where they wanted their ball to go, rather than "I hope I don't screw up . . . ," "I hope I get it right . . . ," "What if I make a mistake . . ."? When Tiger's father communicated to Tiger that he would love him no matter what the final score was, that simple act freed Tiger from worrying about whether he would lose his father's love if he lost the tournament. Consequently, he was free to do his best—and won the tournament.

How many other boys and girls (or men and women, for that matter) would kill to hear their parents say the words to them that Tiger's father told him?

Are you beginning to see why unconditional love is so important for removing success anorexia from our lives? Can you also see how its absence is the primary factor for someone developing success anorexia in the first place?

You may be thinking, "But Noah, if I've never experienced unconditional love or unconditional support, how

---

[1] Sports Illustrated, Tiger Woods: The Making of a Champion, *Bishop Books*, *New York, 1996, pp. 37-38.*

am I supposed to recognize it? How am I going to know when and if it's not there? How am I supposed to get it, or find the people who can love and support me unconditionally?" I'm glad you asked.

There's an old story about a man who asked Michelangelo how he created his masterpiece sculpture of David. Michelangelo replied, "I start with a block of marble and take out everything that isn't David." That's the best description I've ever heard about how to recognize and accept unconditional love in our lives.

To recognize and create an environment of unconditional love and support in our lives, we first need to identify what unconditional love isn't. In other words, if we haven't experienced much unconditional love in our lives, we need to simply start where we are and take the first steps toward where we want to go.

Let's take the first steps together. Please take out your Allowing Success Journal right now and complete these sentences. Don't edit. Don't think. Don't spellcheck. Just finish the sentences. I'll be here when you get back.

1. In my family, love meant . . .

2. When I was young, love meant . . .

3. Love to me means . . .

4. I was taught that love means . . .

5. The love I was shown was . . .

6. I got love when I . . .

7. I didn't get love when I . . .

8. I was punished when I . . .

9. I needed to be loved when I . . .

10. I wished that I had been loved when I . . .

11. I needed my parents' support when I . . .

12. I need the support of others for me to . . .

13. When I feel love, I . . .

14. When I am supported, I can . . .

15. When I feel that love is based upon my performance, I . . .

(I really meant it when I said, "Please take out your journal right now and complete these sentences." If you merely read these sentences and do not do this exercise, you will miss the entire benefit and value of this exercise. Do it. You'll thank me later.)

I know it's not easy to look at some of these issues. That's because most of us tend to minimize what's happened to us. We say things to ourselves like, "It didn't really affect me that much," or "It's no big deal." Paradoxically, we also tend to blow things out of proportion, saying things to ourselves like, "I'll never let anyone get that close to me again," or "They hurt me so much, I can never trust anyone again," or "No one could ever love me."

To really look at the ways we were loved conditionally and expected to perform or conform in order to get love can be painful. I am not denying that. For that reason, many of us never look too closely at our childhood experiences—or, in some cases, never get over them.

Okay. We got through that. What do we do now? Take a look at your list. What does it say? Do you notice a pattern? What were you expected to do? When did you get the love and support you needed? What do you notice about those things in your life today?

For example, I noticed from a very early age that my mother did not feel emotionally supported by my father. I cannot explain how I knew this; I just "knew" it, based on the emotional and psychic information I received at that time. My father was not trained in nor did he have the skills to give the type of emotional support that my mother, as a modern woman, needed and craved. Naturally, since I wanted to make my mother happy, I tried to fill the void left by my father's prolonged absences at work by being my mother's emotional support system. Therefore, I felt that I was needed and appreciated when I emotionally supported my mother and subjugated my emotional needs for hers.

You can guess that this habit continued as I grew older, because I became very used to putting my own emotional, physical and psychic needs after those of my female partner's. A psychologist might say that this is an example of how a "dysfunctional family system" affects someone later in life. While I can't argue with that statement, the question is: how many functional families do you know? Frankly, I have yet to meet the person who has come up to me at one of my seminars and said, "Guess what, Noah? My parents were perfect and did everything right!"

The point is, I could look at what happened in my family and say, "Boy, that was really unfair of my parents and my family to make those demands of me. Why didn't they just love me for who I was?" That's true: it wasn't fair. However, it's also true that life sometimes isn't fair. Not only that, it's also true that my parents did the best they could with the limited tools and knowledge they had (as we all do). The question then becomes: Were my parents raised in an environment of unconditional love and support?

Obviously, neither of my parents were raised in an environment of unconditional love and support. In my parents' case, the environment they grew up in was much, much harsher and more unforgiving than the one in which I was raised. It's also obvious that people cannot demonstrate something in their lives that they do not know how to do. My parents did not "withhold" something that they didn't have in the first place.

It sounds like a cliché to say, "They did the best they could." However, this is precisely the case. Therefore, I could take that information and say, "Oh well, I guess that's the way it goes. Since my parents didn't love me unconditionally, I guess that means no one will ever be able to love or support me unconditionally, and I'll just have to go without it for the rest of my life."

Are you kidding? NO WAY I'm going to settle for that! And neither should you.

Let me put it to you this way: Are your parents the only people in the world who can love you? Is your spouse or are your children the only people from whom you can get love and support? If you believe that they are, that makes it true. However, I challenge that assumption, because it's simply not true that our relatives are the only people who can love and support us unconditionally. In fact, it's pretty obvious that our relatives are often the ones who have the most trouble loving and supporting us unconditionally!

Before we go any further, here's a reality check: No one is going to support or love you unconditionally, in exactly the way you want, perfectly, every single time. To expect someone, anyone, no matter how much they love us, to be there for us every single time, to always say exactly what we need or want to hear, every single time—in short, to love us perfectly and unconditionally—is setting ourselves up for defeat, disillusionment and disappointment.

It is as ridiculous for us to expect others to love us exactly the way we want every single time as it is for others to expect us to show up for them exactly the way they want every single time. Amazingly, the moment we let go of our belief that someone has to change in order for us to be happy, the happier we become, because we then begin to accept reality and stop trying to control things that we cannot control.

Let me ask you a question: Have you ever tried to get others to change by demanding that they change? How did it go? Painful experience has taught most of us that we cannot convince anyone to change by *demanding* that they alter themselves to suit our needs or wishes! There's only one reason human beings ever change: because it suits *them*.

Therefore, the key to accepting unconditional support and surrounding yourself with Loving Mirrors—people who reflect you accurately to yourself (that is, people who can see your Authentic Self)—is to be a Loving Mirror yourself, to yourself and to others. That means you must look in your heart and complete the following statements:

1. Unconditional love to me means . . .

2. If someone were to support me unconditionally, that would mean . . .

3. When someone loves me unconditionally, I . . .

4. If someone were to show up in exactly the way I want . . .

5. Then I might be able to . . .

6. Then I would have the courage to . . .

7. If I did that, I . . .

8. The people in my life who support me are . . .

9. If I could have someone who supported me unconditionally, I . . .

10. They would help me with . . .

11. And then I would learn . . .

12. I can do this because . . .

13. I can allow this because . . .

14. I can let this happen because . . .

I cannot urge you strongly enough to take the time to complete the two simple sentence-completion exercises you'll find in this chapter. Reread this chapter if you need to. Please, for your own sake and the sake of those who care about you, discover your own responses to these vitally important statements of self-examination.

Remember, the role of the counselor, therapist, spouse, parent, brother, sister and friend is to be a Loving Mirror. A true mirror neither adds nor subtracts anything from that which it reflects. Others have their opinions, and most people will be more than happy to share them with you, whether you ask them to or not. However, just because someone else shares his or her opinion with you doesn't mean you have to do anything about it.

When we begin to accept that who we are is our Authentic Self and not our Negative Reflection, something amazing will happen. As if by magic, the people around us will change. What was once okay and acceptable, like having nasty or inconsiderate people around you, will no longer be acceptable to you. What was previously unthinkable—having people in your life who love and support you unconditionally—will become the norm.

I encourage you to remember Who You Really Are. Remember, we humans can never see ourselves as we really are or fully comprehend our true value in life, except as reflected through the eyes of others. When you surround yourself with Loving Mirrors, the world becomes a reflection of the true you, and you will see that it's a beautiful sight to behold.

★ ★ ★

What's the second step to overcoming success anorexia?

10

The Second Step:
Be Willing to Get What You Want

This step addresses why people suffering with success anorexia cannot or do not allow themselves to succeed: They are literally unwilling to succeed because of the temporary dominion of the Negative Reflection over their Authentic Self. The Negative Reflection tells the victim lies such as, "Everyone would be so much happier if you weren't around. . . . You're so selfish. . . . All you ever think of is yourself," etc. When we believe those messages, it is virtually impossible for us to even be willing to succeed, let alone enjoy the fruits of our labors.

Imagine if you had someone looking over your shoulder every minute, analyzing, criticizing, negating your every move. Imagine if they put you down for every action you took. Imagine if that person called you "selfish" and "self-absorbed" if you took any steps toward getting what you want. Wouldn't you do just about anything to make that person stop?

That's exactly what success anorexics do. They unconsciously try to shut out or to appease the Negative Reflection by making sure that they never succeed, thinking that this will stop the ceaseless barrage of criticism. Of course, this may feed and even supplicate the Negative Reflection temporarily, but it is an enormous price for the victims to pay.

The real reason that people starve themselves of success, food, money or anything in life is a belief that doing this will shut out or appease the Negative Reflection. They believe the Negative Reflection when it tells them things such as, "How could you be so selfish . . . Don't you know there are children starving in Africa . . . ?"

Because of their caring and highly sensitive nature, success anorexics honestly want to help the children starving in Africa. They believe that if they just tried hard enough, they really could save the world. They don't realize that it is neither possible nor necessary for one person to save the world. The Negative Reflection makes sure sufferers remains unaware of this, by keeping them isolated in a world of subjectivity and intense self-analysis.

Therefore, to reverse this aspect of the condition, you must develop the willingness to succeed. Let me make a comparison to people with eating disorders. People with eating disorders do not need to learn how to eat. They're perfectly aware that in order to eat, you take a forkful of food, place it in your mouth, chew and swallow.

Similarly, the person struggling with a success disorder knows how to succeed. They've heard all of the tapes, been to all of the seminars and read all of the books. They are drowning in an ocean of how-to-succeed information. However, they are unable to put it to use, because no one's ever told them why they are not succeeding and that they are allowed to succeed.

This behavior completely parallels that of individuals with eating disorders. Those who suffer from eating disorders surround themselves with cookbooks and food, but never let themselves eat. Anorexics will often scrape the crumbs off a nearly empty plate or only eat leftovers. Some anorexics only eat out of garbage cans or dog dishes.

While these behaviors are obviously disturbing, individuals do this because they believe what the Negative Reflection tells them—that they are only worthy of crumbs, leftovers or garbage. Sufferers have no choice but to listen to that voice when they have no other sensory input or data to refute it (in other words, no one in their life who tells them that they're worth more than crumbs).

You'd be amazed at how many people believe they are worth no more than crumbs.

After I discovered success anorexia, I realized that "eating the crumbs of success" is a perfect analogy to what victims of a success disorder do to themselves. They will be surrounded with personal development and self-help literature, but they will be unwilling or unable to use it to actually create a better life for themselves. To use this analogy, they only allow themselves to eat the crumbs and leftovers (or even the garbage) of success.

The pain that success disorder sufferers feel when they know how to succeed, yet are unable to succeed, is difficult to describe. The situation is made even more painful when we realize that this condition has never even been identified in traditional success literature. This makes the individuals not only feel like losers, but that they are the only ones in the world who feel this way.

When I identified this aspect of the condition, I realized that success anorexics do not need more information about how to get what they want, because people struggling with this condition already know how to get what they want (just like an anorexic already knows how to eat). I realized that the key was that the person needed to become *willing* to get what he or she wants.

This almost sounds farcical: How could someone not be willing to get what he or she wants? As I have stated repeatedly in this book, it does not make logical sense to be unwilling to get what you want—but we must remember that we are talking about human beings here, not about creatures that always make logical sense.

Let me give you an example. I grew up in a lower middle-class family, and while we didn't miss any meals, there were many times when we weren't sure if there was going to be food on the table. Money was scarce, even though my father worked eighty to one hundred hours a week.

Friends of our family owned a toy shop in town. I used to go into their store and look longingly at a puppet that was shaped like a raccoon. It was soft and furry, and when I held it, I thought of how happy I would be if I owned that little puppet. Then I would look at the price tag: fifty dollars. I remember thinking that was much more money than my parents would ever be able to spend on me. I would put the little raccoon back on the shelf with a sigh.

Shortly before Christmas that year, my father told me that Santa Claus was a fictional character. (Boy, did I cry when I heard that: My *last chance, gone!* I thought.) On Christmas morning, I came downstairs with a heavy heart. But what do you think I found in one of the boxes? I stared in disbelief as I held the little puppet in my hands. My parents had somehow found a way to buy it for me!

You would think that I would have been overjoyed, ecstatic or at least excited. But I wasn't. The feelings that

I felt were not feelings of joy, but feelings of guilt, sadness and regret—because I knew that it was not Santa who had delivered that toy, but my parents, who (I believed) should not be spending their money on me.

I am in no way blaming my parents for what I felt that day. The point of this story is to demonstrate that if your experience was that getting what you want (in this case, a puppet) caused pain (in the form of feelings of guilt or sadness), do you think you're going to be motivated to get it? Of course not. We've seen that the primary desire of the human being is to avoid pain. Therefore, the second step to overcoming success anorexia is that you must become willing to actually get what you want, and learn that getting what you want does not have to cause pain (to yourself or others).

I want you to think for a moment about the difference between wanting what you want and actually getting what you want. Let's be honest. Isn't it really easier to want what you want than to actually get what you want? Most people go around saying: "I want to win the lottery . . . I want to have more fun . . . I want more time with my family . . ." "I want to go away somewhere . . ." Yet how many of us actually do anything to make those things happen?

Most people would rather complain about what's wrong in their lives than do something to change it. That's because change is what we humans fear most. In fact, change is literally the only thing we can fear. (See chapter 16.) Paradoxically, the only thing we humans can want is also change, because to want something necessarily means altering the current lack of that thing in our lives. For example: Let's say that you want more money, a new car, a better home, nice clothes, increased health, better relationships in your life. What are all these examples of? CHANGE.

Therefore, realize that *what you fear and what you want are exactly the same thing.* It is completely natural for you to feel fear at the prospect of actually getting what you really want. All that is required, if you would really like to get what you want (rather than just wanting it), is that you become willing to get it.

Here are the three steps to becoming willing to actually get what you want.

1. Discover what your true desires are.

The word *desire* comes from a Latin word meaning "of the Lord." Many people believe that their desires are bad or wrong. Some think that it's wrong to even have desires! Whether we like it or not, however, the fact remains that everything we humans do is motivated at its root by a desire of one kind or another. Remember William James's statement that we are run by our passional, and not our logical, nature? What is our passional nature if not desire? If you want an even older source, consider a statement from the Rg Veda, a Hindu story of creation dating back more than five thousand years: "Desire rose from the One in the beginning/Desire was the first seed of mind."

You do not have to be like the millions of people who believe that their desires are bad, wrong or immoral. Everything you see in life had its beginnings in a desire. Nothing exists on Earth that was not born in and of a desire.

In order to allow your desires to manifest, however, you must first find out what they are. You can begin to do this by completing these sentences in your Allowing Success Journal:

1. What I would love to do is _____ because . . .

2. What I would love to learn is _____ because . . .

3. I've always wanted _____ because . . .

4. I need _____ because . . .

5. I need to get _____ because . . .

6. I want to have _____ because . . .

7. I'd love to have _____ because . . .

8. I'd prefer to have _____ because . . .

9. If I could have anything I want, it would be
   _____ because . . .

10. And I'd like it by this date: _____,
    because . . .

If you would like to actually get what you want, you must tell the universe exactly what you want, by when and, most importantly, why. That is why the word "because" appears in every statement in the above exercise. If you do not identify the whys of what you want, all the how-to's in the world will be less than useless to you. Remember, our why-to's and our why-not-to's constitute 90 percent of our ability to get (or not get) anything in life. You can use this knowledge to your advantage by making it known to yourself what your true desires are and why you have them.

Be honest with yourself. You do not have to share your list with anyone else. You may choose, however, to share all or part of your list with one of your Loving Mirrors (that's why that step came first). The purpose of your list is simply for you to realize what already lies inside of you. It's already there; it's aching to come out. It is like a frightened child, however, who has been beaten up by the Negative Reflection for a long, long time.

Be patient and gentle with yourself (for a change). Then, move on to the next step:

2. Examine the benefits and the drawbacks of getting what you want and not getting what you want; in other words, determine your why-to's and your why-not-to's.

There are two sides to getting everything in life: There is the Upside or benefits to getting what you want, and the Downside or drawbacks for getting what you want. For example, most people fantasize about becoming rich and famous. This is because we see TV shows and movies where the lifestyles of the rich and famous seem to be much more glamorous and exciting than our own hum-drum lives. We think, "Boy, if I could only have that or be that, then I'd be happy."

We focus on the Upside because that is the side we are most often shown. We are rarely shown the Downside of fame or wealth, except in tragedies such as the death of Princess Diana. The fact remains that even the famous and the wealthy have problems, face challenges and have to get out of bed in the morning (or at some point in the day) just like the rest of us.

It is simply human nature for the grass to look greener on the other side of the fence. I am not suggesting that you should not want to grow or change, or even that you should not desire fame or wealth. I am suggesting that you determine for yourself both the benefits and the drawbacks of both getting what you want and not getting what you want.

This exercise may be very different from any that you've done in the past. Most of us have been trained to look at why we want to get what we want. I am suggesting that you look at why you are doing what you're currently doing—that is, stopping yourself from getting what you really want—because I guarantee you that there's a darn good reason why you're doing it.

Let's face it: You are doing what you are doing for a reason. You did not wake up one morning and say, "Hmm, I think I'll start not getting what I really want today." What happened was, over time, you learned that getting what you wanted caused you more pain than not getting what you wanted. Since we are biological organisms who are wired to avoid pain, it is next to impossible for you to willingly place yourself in a situation that you believe will cause you more pain than the pain you are currently feeling. This explains why, for many of us, it really is easier to *want* what we want than to actually *get* what we want.

To determine your why-to's and your why-not-to's of getting what you want (versus just wanting it), simply complete the following sentences. Your responses may surprise and even shock you. Complete each statement one, two or even ten times if you need to. Tell yourself the truth.

1. I believe that getting what I want will cause me pain because . . .

2. When I was growing up, I was punished for . . .

3. In my family, success meant . . .

4. In my family, people with money were . . .

5. I learned that happiness meant . . .

6. The price I paid for getting what I wanted was . . .

7. What I get out of starving myself of success is . . .

8. And that helps me because . . .

9. I don't really want to change . . .

10. I feel safe where I am because . . .

11. If I change, that means I'll have to . . .

12. What I really want to do is . . .

Remember, there is a reason for everything we do and don't do. There is nothing you are doing or not doing that is without a reason. The key to change is to uncover our real reasons, not what our logical minds tell us we should or must do.

3. Decide if you are willing to continue to pay the price you are paying to not get what you really want.

This final step is, in a way, the easiest and, in a way, the most difficult. It is the easiest because all it requires of you is to make a decision. You do not have to know exactly what it is you want; you do not have to know how to get it. All that we are talking about here is the answer to the question: Are you willing to get what you really want?

Ironically, this step is also the most difficult because it requires you to make a decision. Only you can decide: Are you willing to change what you are doing? Are you willing to create new habits in your life? Are you willing to ask yourself better questions so that you can go to where you really want to go in life? If you do not have enough reasons, you should by now recognize that no matter how many how-to's of success you know, you will not do what is necessary to allow yourself to get what you want.

Remember, all that we are talking about in this step is the willingness to get what you want. We are not talking about the ways, means or methods of getting what you want. That is what all of those other books in success literature are for. I have shown that if you are not willing to use this information, no matter how smart, talented or capable you are, you will not be able to achieve true, lasting, satisfying success in life.

Life is simply love and law. Life doesn't want you to be miserable, unsuccessful or unhappy. Life is actually more anxious to give you what you want than you are to get it!

Since life is love and law, it can neither break its own law nor do anything about our negative or debilitating beliefs. If you think you're supposed to be unhappy and miserable, then by law, this will be your experience. If you begin to accept the truth that life (also read: God, Higher Power, Infinite Intelligence) wants you to be happy and actually needs you to succeed, then, by the very same law, this too will be your experience.

The decision is yours.

By law, life must reflect back to us whatever we truly believe. (Believe me, this is very good news.) What beliefs do you need to become willing to get what you really want? It's very simple. Here are all the beliefs you need:

1. I am enough.

2. I have enough.

3. I already have all there is.

4. It's okay for me to receive.

5. The universe wants me to be happy.

6. My desires are natural, normal and healthy.

7. Life wants me to receive all the blessings that it has for me and for others.

8. Thank you.

That last one, "Thank you," is the key to the whole equation. If you get nothing else from this book, if you do none of the exercises I've suggested here, do this one thing and your life can't help but change:

When you get up in the morning, say thank you.

When you look in the mirror, say thank you.

When you eat breakfast, say thank you.

When you brush your teeth, say thank you.

When you read the paper, say thank you.

When you watch the news, say thank you.

When you go to bed, say thank you.

If you do this, do you really think you'll be able to keep starving yourself of success?

★ ★ ★

What's the third step to overcoming success anorexia?

11

The Third Step:
Goal-Free Zones

No subject has received more ink in traditional success literature than the subject of goals. What is a goal? Why are they so necessary to achieving success? Most importantly, how can we stop sabotaging our own best efforts in achieving our goals?

Let's begin with a definition of what a goal really is. The word goal comes from a Middle English word, *gol*, meaning "boundary." A goal is "the objective toward which an endeavor is directed." The reason goals are so necessary in achieving success is simple: If we don't know where we are going (our objective), it's impossible to know if we ever got there.

The challenge that persons who are starving themselves of success face is that the goals that they believe
they need to achieve are often simply impossible to
achieve. For example, many of my students have told me
that they believed that it's their job to save the world.
Does that sound like a reasonable goal to you? I like to
call this an example of an impossible goal.

The point is, if you believe that it's your job to save the
world or make everyone happy, you will believe that nothing you do is ever good enough. (See the section in chapter 7 entitled Why We Dismiss Our Own Achievements.)
If you believe that you have to be perfect or save the world
before you're allowed to succeed (or be happy), it's pretty
clear that you're never going to let yourself succeed—
because neither of these objectives is possible to actually
accomplish. Please note, however, that even the presence
of these goals is the hallmark of a highly compassionate,
sensitive person. A selfish person wouldn't care about
cleaning up the planet or helping others, would they?

Anorexics, whether they are starving themselves of food
or success, will often try to fix the problems of the world
by going without—that is, by starving themselves of food
or success. When their efforts fail to fix the world, as they
surely must (because fixing the world is an impossible
goal), they now have more evidence that they are failures.

Why do anorexics believe that it's their job to save the
world? Simply because they've been told this over and

over again by their Negative Reflection. In addition, it's a great way to keep themselves from succeeding. (If you have a goal like saving the world, where would you even begin?)

Many of a success anorexic's goals, like saving the world or being perfect, are impossible to achieve. Remember, these are not necessarily our conscious thoughts. We don't read books and go to seminars to learn how to save the world! This is just a representation of the scale of achievement many of us feel we have to accomplish in order to be worthwhile.

This is also a brilliant strategy used by the Negative Reflection to keep us from focusing upon our own (lack of) success and happiness in life. When you're constantly focused upon the troubles of the world, it's easy to forget that you don't have enough money to pay the rent, are alone all the time, etc. It's also a good strategy to keep yourself from taking the steps to create the life that you really want.

Again, I do not want to make it sound as if success anorexics have their heads in the clouds. Quite the reverse is true. Success anorexics are more aware of the problems of the world than most people. If anything, they are too aware of these problems. They believe that these problems are literally their responsibility, and that they do not or will not deserve success until and unless they fix them.

The belief that any individual can or should save the world is simply false. There is just no way around that fact. (Believe me, I would change it, too, if I could.) The belief that one person can save the world is simply a lie that the Negative Reflection tells its victims—who, iron-ically, are the very members of society who have both the ability and the desire to help solve the problems!

This creates a tremendously painful struggle inside the victim: "I know I could help people, if I could just learn how to help myself; but since I can't help myself, I'm probably no good to anyone else." This twisted logic keeps the victim isolated and the Negative Reflection at the helm. What is needed, once again, is to teach stu-dents that no one human being can or even should try to save the world. It's simply not their job, nor can it even be done.

One of the ways to do this is by using *Goal-Free Zones* in your life. A Goal-Free Zone is a time, a place or a cir-cumstance when you do not do anything, when you sim-ply ARE. A Goal-Free Zone, as its name suggests, is a time and place where there are no goals, no deadlines, no responsibilities and nothing that needs to be done or must be done.

What was your first thought when you read that para-graph? Was it, *YES!* Or was it, *Oh no!* Goal-Free Zones are actually one of the most slippery parts of this teaching, because setting and keeping them are not easy as it might appear. Success anorexics have taken more goal-setting courses and workshops than anyone on the planet. They know how to set goals! However, they almost never allow themselves to manifest or enjoy the simple pleasures of life, simply because they believe that they should only have them when all of their goals are fulfilled.

You need to release yourself from this tortuous logic, because it's simply not true that you only get to relax when you're perfect and the world is whole. If that were the case, nobody would ever get to relax.

You need to create for yourself a setting where you are free both from the goals that you've set for yourself and the ones that you've inherited from others. This is vital, because you need to experience and understand that your worth, value and meaning do not come from your achievements, your accolades or how many awards you win, or from what you do for others.

Success anorexics have often been well-praised for their achievements and accomplishments. They've won awards, earned the best grades and done the best performances. Yet they receive very little inner satisfaction from these accolades, because they honestly believe that anyone could have done it. *Hello?* We need to wake you up to see that what you have done and who you are are more than good enough. You do NOT need to save the world in order to be worthy of success, happiness and pleasure in life.

Let me give you an example. I moved to Los Angeles in the late 1980s with one purpose in mind: to become a movie star. Mind you, I didn't want to be an actor. No, that wouldn't have been good enough. I had to be a movie star. After I landed the very first role that I auditioned for, I felt certain that this was my destiny.

I waited another six months before landing my next role. Believe me, the parts I won were not exactly worth waiting for. After four years of painfully long stretches between roles, and parts that did not make Steven Spielberg give me a call, I moved back to Maine. Amazingly, Hollywood didn't fold up its doors. Later, I realized that my insistence that I become a movie star made me forget one little detail: that you have to become an actor first.

Back in Maine, I also realized something I had never admitted in all those years in Hollywood: I was sick of acting! I'd been performing onstage since I was three years old (my father ran a local theater company, so my brother and I would entertain cast members during rehearsal breaks), and the fun had simply gone out of it. I was tired of reading other people's lines; I just wanted to be myself. However, in my zealous pursuit of an impossible goal, I never devoted myself to the craft of acting. Sure, I took acting classes—but I felt that I was above them and was just waiting for my big break. (Geez, with an attitude like that, I wonder why it never came?)

After leaving Hollywood, I noticed something fascinating when I watched interviews with people we call movie stars. They rarely talk about how glamorous and wonderful their lives are. Instead, they talk about their work, their craft, the movie or the Broadway show they're performing in. Most of all, they talk about the people they work with. I noticed that they all seemed to have one thing that I lacked: a love of acting!

It isn't hard to see why I didn't become a movie star. Not only did I not do what it takes to make it happen, I didn't like what I was doing. Not exactly a recipe for success!

The point of this story is to show you that success is not something mysterious; it is neither a matter of chance nor of luck. Success occurs as a result of doing what you love combined with the awareness of precisely where you are going, and taking the appropriate steps along the path to your destination.

That's why Goal-Free Zones are so necessary. Without an awareness of where we are going, how will we know when we get there? What if where we're going is not where we want to end up? How can we enjoy the journey if we don't even want to visit the destination?

A Goal-Free Zone enables you to take a breath. To stop. To listen to yourself and your inner longings. To ask questions that you normally wouldn't ask, like: "Where am I going? What am I doing? What is the purpose of my work? What's my reason for being on Earth? Am I going in the direction I really want to go?"

There are no right answers to these questions. Not only that, but your answers will change over time. A

Goal-Free Zone gives you the opportunity to look at these questions as you are planting flowers in your garden, walking in a field, playing golf, cleaning your car or baking a cake.

Notice that these are all activities. I did say earlier in this chapter that a Goal-Free Zone is a time and place where you don't do anything. However, that is only partially true. A more precise definition of a Goal-Free Zone is a time and place where you stop pursuing your goals for a while.

Let's face it. For some of us, relaxing means lying on a beach. For others, lying on the beach is anything but relaxing. Relaxing can mean playing tennis. For others, it's playing the piano, playing cards or playing Frisbee with your dog. Other methods of relaxation include:

- taking a nap
- baking cookies
- washing your car
- raking leaves
- coloring in a coloring book
- painting
- making love
- in-line skating
- waterskiing

- writing

- taking apart a computer and putting it back together

- fishing

- jogging

- biking

- hiking

- reading

- getting/giving a massage

You get the idea. These are only a few ideas of what you could do in your Goal-Free Zone. Write in some of your own ideas. You don't have to sit around like a bump on a log to be in a Goal-Free Zone.

Sherri, one of my students, called me one day and said, "Noah, I'm on vacation and I'm thinking about what you told me. I just realized that the whole time I was supposed to have been on vacation, I've been running around, doing something—I haven't stopped for five minutes! I'm sitting here trying to do a Goal-Free Zone and every time I stop, I think of ten things I should be doing! I keep saying to myself, 'Why did Noah have to teach me about these damn Goal-Free Zones now?'" By this time, of course, we were both laughing hysterically.

I did not say that it was easy to set or live in Goal-Free Zones. We are trained from a young age to do, do, do; that "A rolling stone gathers no moss," "Idle hands are the devil's playground" and so forth. I do not refute that this step requires a certain kind of willpower; ironically, however, it is the willingness to stop doing so much.

You will benefit in subtle yet profound ways from using Goal-Free Zones. You will gradually learn that the world doesn't come crashing to a halt when you stop for twenty to thirty minutes a day. Ironically, you'll also find that you'll be able to get more done in less time when you use Goal-Free Zones, because you'll be able to hear the messages coming to you from your subconscious mind—messages that are drowned out by the incessant "busyness" that so many of us are used to. Our subconscious mind provides answers to questions in unexpected ways, because it works in a nonlogical, nonlinear fashion. However, the subconscious mind is like a shy playmate—it must feel safe to come out and play.

People often ask me "How do I set Goal-Free Zones?" There are really two ways to do it:

1. Decide on a certain time of day for your daily Goal-Free Zone.

For example, you might say, "Okay, from 9:30 to 10:00, I'm going to be in my Goal-Free Zone." Announce it to your family and friends, if necessary. Enforce it by making sure that the people in your life respect it, too.

The other way to do it is:

2. When you find, during your day, that you're starting to feel upset or overwhelmed, or that you're trying to do too many things at once—STOP. Take a breath. Declare out loud, "Okay! We are now entering a Goal-Free Zone."

I found that I'm most comfortable using the second strategy. Whenever I start to feel that there's a million things that have to be done yesterday, I stop, take a breath and say out loud, "Okay! We are now entering a Goal-Free Zone." This makes me simply STOP. (Notice that I didn't say this was easy; but believe me, if I can do it, you can do it, too.)

My personal favorite Goal-Free Zone activity? Taking a nap. A nap gives me a built-in Goal-Free Zone; it's absolutely certain that I can't strive to achieve anything while I'm asleep! Plus, I've found that taking a twenty-minute nap every four to six hours can add another two to four hours to my day.

Using Goal-Free Zones may feel awkward, even wrong, to you at first. This is completely normal. If you've spent your whole life doing, doing, doing, it's going to feel weird to stop doing. Hang in there. After a while, doing nothing in particular won't feel so bad after all.

★ ★ ★

What's the fourth step to overcoming success anorexia?

12

The Fourth Step:
Goal-Replacement Surgery

D o you know what your potential is?
Have you ever felt that you're not
living up to it? If you said no to the
first question and yes to the second, you're
not alone.

The word *potential* has probably caused
more cases of success anorexia than any other
word in the English language. That's because
victims are painfully aware that they are not
living up to it, whatever it is. It's as though
there's a bar that you're trying to jump over,
but every time you leave the ground, somebody raises it on you. When we feel that we're
not living up to our potential, we often work
harder to prove that we're trying to live up to

it. However, if we don't even know what our potential is, how will we know when we're living up to it?

This phenomenon is highly visible in the arena of competitive sports. It is sad to see how many players and athletes never live up to their potential. Vin Scully, the venerable sports broadcaster, once said, "There may be no more frightening word to a player or coach [of a sports team] than the word 'potential.'"

The issue of potential, and the damage the idea can produce, led me to develop an exercise called **Goal-Replacement Surgery**. I coined this term when I realized two things:

1. The victim of success anorexia needs to stop setting so many goals (that's the reason for the Goal-Free Zones of the previous chapter); however,

2. It is impossible for a person to have no goals.

It is simply not possible for a human being to not want things. We human beings are goal-driven creatures. We see or think about something that we want, then we take steps to get it. That's who we are and how we operate; it's how we are built.

Soon after I discovered success anorexia, I realized that it was imperative for students to learn that their worth does not depend upon their outer achievements, their awards or accolades, whether they save the world or become a movie star. However, I also realized that the

nature of human beings is that we are goal-driven creatures. Therefore, I realized that while recovering success
anorexics could not be without goals—because that's
really not possible or realistic—they would need to adapt
or shift the goals that they believed they must accomplish in order to be worthy of success.

In short, I realized that recovering success anorexics
would have to replace their impossible goals with ones that
made more sense for their happiness, well-being and fulfillment. That is the reason for Goal-Replacement Surgery.

It's amazing how many people have next to no idea
what they really want or what would make them happy.
These individuals are by no means lazy, incompetent or
lacking in ambition. They are simply not letting themselves succeed. What they lack is not intelligence or persistence, but permission to succeed.

They have spent their whole lives focused on trying to
make the world right and everyone else happy while
neglecting their own happiness. When they learn that
making everyone else happy is an impossible goal, and
that they couldn't do this no matter how perfect they
were, the effect is similar to that of a blind person seeing
the sky for the first time.

The success anorexic's life has been spent trying to
do what is, by definition, impossible: making everyone
else happy. When they learn that making everyone else
happy actually is impossible, they say, "You mean I'm

not a failure? You mean I'm *not* no good? You mean I *don't* have to make everyone else happy to be worthy of success?"

Yes. That's exactly what I mean. Again, I want to stress that I in no way tell students what they should do or what they should want, nor do I tell anyone what success should mean to them. I do not give recommendations based upon my opinions or experience as to what they should want or strive for. Students often ask me, "Well, what do you think I should do?"

This question is really a test of whether or not I trust them to make the right decision. It's vitally important that I communicate to them that *I* know that *they* know what's right for *them*. I say something like, "Well, you know what's best for you much better than I do. What do you think?" Or, "What do you want to do?" Or, "What do you feel is best for you?"

They don't always like my response at first. That's because they're accustomed to trying to please everyone but themselves. Many students have told me later that those very questions helped them to grow and learn what they really wanted, because it was the first time that someone had trusted them to know what they really wanted for themselves, and didn't try to tell them what they should do.

Here, then, are the steps for Goal Replacement Surgery. Take out your journal again. (Yes, I mean right now.)

1. Write down what your current (impossible) goals are. Then write your responses to these sentence-completion exercises:

   I feel that I must . . .

   I have to . . .

   I should . . .

   They're counting on me to (and write down whoever "they" are) . . .

   It's imperative that I . . .

   I can't . . .

   If I don't _____, then . . .

   If I don't _____, that means that I'll . . .

   If I don't _____, then my parents will say . . .

   If I don't _____, then I'll be a failure because . . .

2. Stop. Look at your list.

   Take a deep breath and pause. What did you just write? Did that come from you—or are those messages coming from someone else?

3. Ask yourself, "Is this really what I want to do, or did this goal come from someone or someplace else?"

Listen. Then write the answer to that question, for each message on your list.

4. If the goals you've internalized aren't really yours (but someone else's), ask yourself, "What do I really want to do/learn/share?"

Go back to the exercises in chapter 9 on Unconditional Support. Do the exercises again, keeping in mind all of these other messages that you've just unearthed. Why do them again? Because now you'll have realized that many of the messages you've heard about what you have to do and must do are not coming from you at all.

It is no one else's business what your dreams, desires and goals are. If you choose to share your dreams and plans with other people, remember that whomever you will share your ideas with will undoubtedly share their opinions with you, whether you ask for them or not. This applies particularly to family members, because they are the people who don't want to see you take risks or get hurt.

When people share their opinions with you (as they are bound as if by law to do), I suggest that you use the technique utilized by Franklin Delano Roosevelt. FDR was one of the most popular, beloved presidents in American history. It is no coincidence that he was also a superb listener. He would listen to the opinions of senators and congressmen on different sides of every issue, each one receiving FDR's rapt attention. By the end of the meeting, every senator and congressman was certain that Roosevelt saw it his way and would do exactly as the senator or congressman had suggested. Of course, FDR would then proceed to do exactly what he'd planned to do all along, regardless of what anyone had said.

I've found this strategy to be exquisitely effective in dealing with people, particularly family members. It's absolutely certain that those who care the most about our well-being will never want us to take any risks. However, it's also certain that if we never take any risks, we can never build anything of lasting value.

You will find it easier to listen to the opinions of others when you realize that everyone is bound to share their opinions with you. Stop expecting others to agree with you. Instead, expect them to offer their opinion, and get excited when it's different from yours. You will find something magical happening: You'll find that you can listen to people and not do a damn thing to make them happy. Just the simple process of listening gives most people what they want: the chance to be heard. If you can give people that, you will be giving them the greatest human gift of all.

★ ★ ★

What's the fifth step to overcoming success anorexia?

13

The Fifth Step: Two-a-Days

Have you ever noticed that, as a society, our in-boxes are getting fuller and fuller? How many items are there on your to-do list today? Five? Ten? Twenty? More? When you don't get all of them done in a day, what do you do or say to yourself? If you're like many of the people I've worked with, your internal dialogue probably goes something like this:

"You bungling so-and-so, why can't you get more done in a day? Don't you know there are more things you have to do, don't you know your brother (or sister or whoever it is you compare yourself to) would be able to get this done in a day, and probably more . . . ?" And so on.

The point is that most of us tell ourselves that we have to do more today than we could possibly get done in a day. Yet, at the same time, we don't believe that we can accomplish what we really want to do with our lives. It's as if we're hiding our true selves behind a mountain of to-do's that don't really take us closer to realizing or actualizing our dreams—if we even let ourselves know what those dreams are!

What is the solution to this problem? Well, we could try to ignore it and hope it goes away. Or we could keep doing what we're doing and hope for a different result. But you and I both know that these solutions will lead you exactly nowhere.

That's where **Two-a-Days** come in. I have found it to be the most effective technique I've ever used to remove that feeling of "not-enough-ness" when it comes to my in-box (and indeed, my life).

What are Two-a-Days? A Two-a-Day is an activity or series of activities that you enjoy doing, that you do twice a day, once in the morning and once at night (or in the afternoon). Why twice? The reason is that we very often set lofty goals for ourselves without ever taking the steps to do them. When we think about doing something just twice in a day, we can make that mountain more like a gently sloping hill.

Now, it may sound almost funny to you to think about scheduling doing something that brings you joy and pleasure. However, I invite you to think about it. When was the last time you actually DID something you enjoy doing (rather than just think about doing it)? When was the last time you got something done and actually felt the satisfaction of having done it? Come to think of it, when was the last time you did something you enjoyed—and didn't feel guilty about doing it?

In our culture, we are often taught to associate feeling good with the feeling we call guilt. When we look at it this way, it's almost comical. Our basic need to feel good and to derive pleasure from what we do is compounded by the guilty feeling that comes the moment we actually feel good about doing it! No wonder so many of us are busily pushing away the very thing we want most in life.

Conversely, we are also taught that if we're working hard with our nose to the grindstone, we are somehow doing something worthy and that we're somehow earn-ing points to our heavenly reward. Has anyone ever seen a score card for these points? Let me let you in on a little secret: No one is keeping score except you! There are no extra points for suffering. You don't earn extra credit by working hard or putting your nose to the grindstone. (You'll probably just end up with a ground-up nose.)

I am not suggesting that we stop working hard or that we should advocate sloth as a way of life. I am suggesting, however, that often the harder we work, the more we tend to push away the very thing we want most.

Remember, ideas about hard work were taught to us by well-meaning parents and teachers who really wanted the best for us. Unfortunately, many of us became really, really good at not allowing positive feelings and experiences in; at working hard for almost no gain, recognition or pleasure; and at feeling guilty the moment something good happens to us.

Obviously, feelings and behaviors such as those just described are not conscious thoughts. No one goes around saying, "Gee, I'm happy, so I'd better feel guilty now." No parent consciously teaches their child to feel guilty for feeling good. Rather, what happens is that these ideas creep up on us when we are not aware of them. We notice that when something good happens to us, we feel weird, strange, even scared—but we're at a loss to explain this phenomenon.

What we usually do in that case is to rid ourselves of any success we've gained, in order to reach our own internal level of comfort and safety. (The second book in this series deals with this phenomenon in much more detail.) The message in our heads goes something like this:

"If I'm happy and doing something I enjoy, that means I must not be working very hard. And if I'm not working hard, that means I don't deserve all the good things that are happening to me. What if someone comes along and takes away what I have? Maybe I should just give it back before someone takes it away from me. (And one thing

I'd really better not do is let anyone know just how much I really like myself!)"

A Simple Exercise That Can Make All the Difference

Where do Two-a-Days fit into all this? The answer is simple. If the problem is that you have not felt allowed to take the time to do the things you enjoy doing, and you feel guilty about your own pleasure and fulfillment, the solution is to do the reverse of what you've been doing.

Oh sure, Noah. And pigs will fly next Tuesday.

Please be gentle with yourself. I am not suggesting that these changes are as easy as I'm making them sound. But you know as well as I do that if we keep doing what we're doing, we're going to keep getting what we're getting. Doesn't it make sense to just start something new . . . and see what happens?

Let's take it one simple step at a time. First, complete the following sentences:

1. If I had enough time, I would . . .

2. If I had enough money, I would . . .

3. If money were no object, I would . . .

4. If time were not an issue, I would . . .

5. If I had the chance, I would . . .

6. I always wanted to . . .

7. What gives me a lot of pleasure is . . .

8. I'd love to learn . . .

9. I'd love to . . .

10. It's always a pleasure when I . . .

Okay. You're probably speed-reading through this and not filling in those blanks. Do me just one favor. Take a deep breath. Now, go to your desk and get a pen. Write in just one response to each of these sentence beginnings. Yes, I mean write them right here in this book. (Hey, you bought it; that means it's yours to write in. Of course, if you're reading this in a bookstore, this could present a problem.)

Do it. Complete the sentences. Write in your journal if you really want to go to town on them. I'll be right here when you get back.

★ ★ ★

Did you find at least one Two-a-Day activity, something you really like and enjoy and feel a lot of pleasure and satisfaction doing?

Great. Now, what I want you to do is DON'T DO IT.

"What?! You just told me to write them down and now you want me to not do it? Are you crazy?

Stay with me on this one.

You see, if this were an ordinary self-help book, what you would have read there is that you need to schedule time to do these things you enjoy doing and then have fun doing them.

Well, in case you haven't noticed by now, this is not an ordinary self-help book.

The reason I did not say that you should go out and do these Two-a-Days is that, quite frankly, I know all the tricks the Negative Reflection plays on its victims (because I've done them all to myself!). You see, when I started to overcome success anorexia, I wrote these lists of all the things I like to do, like play golf, make love and read a book (not necessarily in that order). Then I would go right back to doing what I always did—not doing them!

That's why I created the concept of Two-a-Days. What I'd like you to realize is that you are doing everything you are doing—and not doing everything you're NOT doing—for a reason. The reason you're doing or not doing them is that, for whatever reason, you believe it's better to do what you're doing and better to not do what you're not doing. (Still with me?)

If I were to tell you to just go out there and start doing those things you like doing (but have been avoiding doing), what would you do? Probably say, "Some day I'll get around to it"—and keep doing what you've always done, which is not doing them.

That's why I'm telling you that, after you write down those things you really like to do, the one thing you can't do is do them.

That's right. I said DON'T DO THEM.

Does that sound weird to you? What are you thinking now?

Are you thinking something like this: "Who does this guy think he is, to tell me not to do what I like to do? I'll show you—I'm going out and doing them!"

Did you notice how, the moment I said you couldn't go out and do those things you like to do, you instantly felt *deprived* of them—even when you weren't doing them just a few minutes ago? Isn't it amazing that when someone else tells you you can't do it, you get ornery, but when you tell yourself you can't do it, you believe it?

You see, the moment I told you that you couldn't go out and do them, you said to yourself, "Hey, why should I be deprived of those things? I deserve them just as much as anyone else! Why the heck should I not have those things?"

There is no reason at all you shouldn't have the things you enjoy. None whatsoever.

Are you beginning to see what's happening here? You yourself have been the only one who has deprived yourself of the things you enjoy. But when someone else tries to deprive you of them, you get your dander up and say, "Give me that back!"

Yes! That's precisely how I want you to feel about yourself. The point is, you deserve only the best. You deserve to enjoy yourself and have fun. And there is no reason at all for you to deprive yourself of the things you enjoy.

Uh-oh. I think I just heard some of you say, "But you don't understand. . . . I don't have the money . . . or the time . . . or know anyone who can help me get the things I want. . . ."

Wait a minute. Didn't we just go through this? Don't you remember that I said you were supposed to NOT go out and do those things you wanted to do? That you were supposed to make sure you DON'T let yourself enjoy yourself today or be happy with your accomplishments?

"Who does he think he is, telling me not to have what I want or appreciate my own accomplishments?"

Bingo! Who indeed?

Do you see what's happening here? This is the eternal paradox of human nature: We will deny ourselves until the cows come home, but if someone else tries to take away what we've got or what we want, we will fight like tigers to get it or keep it. It's just like this: You can make fun of your own family, but if someone else makes fun of your family, watch out!

Are you starting to grasp the concept?

The point is, I want you to look at all the ways you've been denying yourself, and then play this little game with yourself: Pretend someone told you you couldn't have it or do it. What would you do then?

If you're like me, your dander would instantly rise up and say, "Hey, who do you think you are? If I want that thing, I'll have it . . . now!"

I've practically made a career out of doing what others said I couldn't or shouldn't be doing—even if they never said it to my face, and even if I was the only one who said it couldn't be done. That's how and why I wrote the first edition of this book in only two weeks (actually I wrote it in five days, took four days off, and edited it for five more days, for a total of two weeks). I made a bet with myself that if I started on Monday morning, the book couldn't be done by Friday at 5:00 P.M. *Oh yeah*, I said. *Try me*.

Guess what? The sucker was done at 4:53 P.M. Friday afternoon. (Sure, it took a few eighteen-hour days, but I told you I was ornery.)

I would bet the farm that you are just as ornery as I am. I invite you to learn from my mistakes and stop trying to get yourself to do something you just don't feel comfortable doing. If you are anywhere near as stubborn as I am, you have something inside of you that says you can do it when others tell you you can't. (Most of my clients and students who who fit this description.) Play a game with yourself that goes something like this:

Make a bet with yourself that you can't do something twice a day that you really enjoy doing, once in the morning and once at night or in the afternoon. Or make a wager that you can't even find three things that you like doing! Bet yourself that you can't take any pleasure in your accomplishments. Of course, if you have already identified more than five things you really like to do, make a bet with yourself that says, "I bet you can't even do two of them in a week." See how long it takes you to do all five!

The point of Two-a-Days is not to give you one more thing to stress you out. It's to play with the idea that we are victims of circumstances beyond our control. I say that we have much more control over the events in our lives than we are led to believe. It's handy, however, to say and believe that events or circumstances (and even people) beyond our control are controlling us. That way, we don't have to take any responsibility to change the things we don't like. I invite you to take a different tactic: Use your imagination and your sense of playfulness to get back on the horse of life and ride it for all it's worth.

Who knows? After a while, you might even find yourself enjoying what you do.

(But whatever you do, don't let anyone pay you lots of money for doing it!)*

★★★

What's the sixth step to reversing success anorexia?

---

*This was another statement to jolt you out of your "deprive-me" thinking habits and behavior patterns. Did it work?

14

The Sixth Step: Find Your "No"

Once upon a time, it was very difficult for me to say no to people. Since I wanted everyone to like me, I figured that the best way to do that would be to try and be all things to all people. If someone asked me to do something, I immediately said yes, even though I often regretted it later. I was so desperate for people's approval, I was terrified of anyone being angry or upset with me.

There were several problems with this strategy. One, I couldn't figure out what everyone else wanted, and it often changed from day to day; two, trying to be all things to all people left me mentally, physically and emotionally exhausted; and three, it didn't work. In fact, it produced precisely the *opposite* effect of what I wanted. Not only did I not get everyone else to like me, I actually managed to alienate a lot of people, because they could see that I was a "yes-man" who tried to make himself into whatever anyone else wanted him to be.

This was particularly evident in my relationships with women. I tried so hard to impress them that I would simply change my personality to suit whoever I was with to try and make them happy. It doesn't take a rocket scientist to figure out why that strategy was so effective in keeping women away from me! The fact is women (and men as well) can sense when someone is not being genuine with them. Frankly, most of us are conditioned not to trust anyway, so that when we sense someone isn't being totally honest with us, it merely makes us that much more suspicious.

The point of all this is to help you learn from my mistakes. I invite you to do something that it took me years to learn: **find your no.** What do I mean by that? Finding your no means that you must come to the point in your life where you can say no to people and mean it. In the words of one of my friends, "'No' is a complete sentence."

Why is that so hard for many of us? It's very simple. We are human beings, and every human being wants only three things: approval, attention and appreciation. (See chapter 16.) You could say that what we all really want boils down to one word: acceptance. Many of us equate the word *no* with "I don't like you" or "I don't approve of you" or even "You're a bad person." I know that may sound harsh, but think about it: Weren't these some of the messages you heard (implicitly or explicitly) when you were told *no* while you were growing up?

Many of us would rather die than hurt someone else. Since we believe that saying no to others would hurt their feelings and cause them pain (like what we felt when we were children), we feel incredibly guilty saying no to others. We don't want anyone else going through the kind of pain we went through. My two responses to that line of thinking are:

One, it shows that you are a very compassionate person. Two, you're wrong.

When you say no to someone, it does not have to mean that you are saying "I don't like you" or "I disapprove of you" or "You are a bad person." Think about it: How often are you really saying those things when you say no? Very, very rarely, I'd wager.

What does no really mean? No is simply an expression of refusal or disagreement with that which has been presented. Let's use an example and bring this to its logical conclusion. I want you to think about this question: Are you sure you really want *everyone* to like you? That means junkies, murderers, people who commit violent crimes. Do you really want these people to like you?

Of course not, you say. That part was easy. We've just eliminated a whole bunch of people whose approval you don't want or need. What about other people: say, salespeople, politicians, and other people who are trying to convince you to buy their products (which might be themselves)? Do you want all of these people to like you?

No, clearly not. Each of these people has an agenda.

Ahh, now we come to the heart of it, the reality behind the illusion. Is it not true that every human being you will ever meet has her or his own agenda?

"But," you say, "what about all those generous people out there? What about the firefighters, police officers, surgeons, doctors and ministers, who devote all of their time and energy to helping and giving to other people? And what about me? That's all I do every day! Are you saying that I have my own agenda?"

Of course you do.

We must look under the surface to what is really going on inside you and everyone else on Earth. Let's take firefighters, who not only risk their lives to save others, but often volunteer their time so that they're not even being paid for putting their life before yours. What agenda could these men and women possibly have, you say? These are the most noble and giving, generous and kind persons in the world. Indeed, they are. And that is precisely his agenda.

Remember, just because someone has an agenda (which really means what they want) doesn't mean they can't be generous, kind and giving, too. In fact, for many people, being generous and giving to others IS their agenda. Not everyone is inspired or motivated by the simple end of gaining a lot of money.

That, is precisely how and why to find your no.

How and Why to Find Your "No"

Finding your no consists of four simple steps:

1. Discover what you really want and Who You Really Are.

2. Express that.

3. Let others do the same.

4. Repeat.

Let's examine each step in turn.

1. Discover what you really want and Who You Really Are.

This step is much, much easier said than done. Practically every self-help and inspirational book ever written attempts to help people work this step. Not only that, but Who You Really Are is not a static thing; it is not something you do once and then say, "Okay, I discovered who I really am. What's for lunch?"

We are constantly re-creating ourselves at every moment of our existence. The challenge is that most people don't realize that Who They Really Are is not set in stone; Who We Really Are adjusts according to our dreams, demands and decisions, which can change every single day.

The easiest and simplest way I know to discover what you really want and Who You Really Are is to complete the following sentences:

1. If I could do anything I wanted, I would . . .

2. If I could be who I wanted to be, I would . . .

3. If I could play any part, it would be . . .

4. If I could help people, I would . . .

5. If I knew myself, I would . . .

6. When I discover what I want to do, I will . . .

7. The purpose of my life is to . . .

8. I am here on Earth to . . .

Do it. Go ahead. Complete these sentences. Yes, I mean right here (and write here) in your Allowing Success Journal. I'll be right here when you finish.

These questions are breathtakingly simple. Yet they are also some of the deepest questions known to humankind. We have striven to answer them for thousands of years collectively and possibly for decades individually. Just keep going. Keep doing it. The reward is in the asking, not always the answer. (For a list of other resources to help you discover what you really want and Who You Really Are, please see the section For Further Learning.)

2. Express what you really want and Who You Really Are.

Now we come to the tricky part. You see, the real challenge in life is not to know or discover Who We Really Are. We really already know that. It's just that we spend most of our time denying it!

If you were to walk around today and express Who You Really Are, what would happen? Would people laugh at you? Call you crazy—or worse? Would they lock you up and throw away the key? These are just some of the irrational fears we feel when we even consider being and expressing Who We Really Are (our Authentic Self). The amazing thing, however, is that when we are simply ourselves, nothing at all special happens. The world doesn't end. The earth doesn't stop revolving. The sun still comes up.

The problem is, we just don't believe that.

Have you ever asked yourself where all these fears about expressing our Authentic Selves came from? The answer is so obvious, we frequently miss it. Most of us were taught to feel shame or guilt when we expressed our true, Authentic Selves. When we were happy, joy-filled, full of childlike enthusiasm and love of nature, trusting of everyone we met, and we expressed that, it was okay for a while. Slowly, but surely, however, we were taught that it was not right to trust everybody, that the world was not always a safe place, that people often made fun of us if we were too happy, that the safest thing to do was to be nice and do what the teacher told you to do. When you think about it, it's amazing that anyone has the courage to do anything creative at all!

For this we should not blame our parents, teachers or caretakers. They really did the best they could and really did want what was best for us. The challenge is that what they thought was best for us may not have been what's truly best for us. We can realize that, over time, many of us learned that the price for being and expressing who we really were was simply too high.

The point is, it was smart of you to not express that childlike exuberance and trust of everyone you met. It was a good decision to try and be nice and do what the teacher told you to do. It was a good thing that you learned to get in step with what other people wanted you to do (for example, when learning to cross the street or how to drive a car).

Now, however, you are an adult. You have a decision to make. You have the power to say yes to what you like and no to what you do not like. You have suffered and struggled long enough. There are no more points to be earned. If you want to make a change, why not save yourself and others a lot of time, energy and pain, and simply let yourself *be?*

Expressing Who You Really Are—your Authentic Self—is not always easy. However, life seems to be set up so that the only way for us to manifest our true desires is to do just that, almost like there is a test of courage and inner strength that must be passed in order for life to hand out its rewards.

It is time for you to reap the harvest of all your years of hard work and labor. Let yourself succeed and enjoy the bounty of harvest that life has laid out for you. To help you do this, please complete the following sentences about why you deserve success:

1. I can let myself win now because . . .

2. I can say no to what I don't want now because . . .

3. I can say yes to what I want now because . . .

4. I can be who I want to be now because . . .

5. I can let myself succeed now because . . .

6. I am allowed to succeed now because . . .

7. I let myself succeed now because . . .

Now we come to the third step in this delightful process:

3. Let others be and express Who They Really Are.

This step is, at the same time, trickier and easier than Step 2. It is often much easier for us to see the uniqueness and beauty in another person than in ourselves. That is because when you look in a mirror, you can never see yourself as you really are. All we can ever see of ourselves is in two dimensions. Other people, however, can see us in all four dimensions (including time). Perhaps that is why nature gave us each other.

In any case, we must let others be and express their Authentic Selves too, if we expect to allow ourselves to be and express our own. Jesus pointed this out when he reminded us to "Do unto others as you would have them do unto you." Remember that it is not necessary for you to agree with or support everything everyone else is doing to live and let live. You wouldn't support your children going on drugs, would you? There is a fine line between saying "Anything goes" and "I love you for Who You Really Are" (see chapter 9).

The easiest way to help yourself express your Authentic Self is to use these three simple phrases:

What I want for myself, I want for others.

What I want for myself is . . .

What I want for others is . . .

(Fill in the blanks with what you really want for
others.)

You may find, for example, that what you really want
for yourself is "to be happy" or "love" or "to know peace."
You may also be surprised to discover that that is exactly
what you want for other people, too. When you make it
into a simple phrase that you can always have near you,
you will remember that being Who You Really Are is
both easier and harder, at the same time, than not doing
so. (This is one of the eternal paradoxes of human life:
being Who You Really Are is at once more difficult and
easier than anything else we will ever attempt.)

Finally, the last step of the process of finding your no is:

4. Repeat.

Remember that Who You Really Are, your Authentic
Self, is not a static entity. It is not a point at which you
arrive and say, "Done!" It is both a process and a product,
a journey and a destination, a means and a never-ending
end. It is something you and I will be engaged in for the
rest of our time here on Earth—perhaps longer!

Expect yourself to arrive, and once you are there, to
say, "Is that it?" Growth, change and, in fact, frustration
and the desire to experience more are all hard-wired into

the human organism. We humans are simply among the most restless creatures on Earth. Allow yourself the freedom to be and to do, to move and to stay still, to stop and to start, to begin and to end. These are the freedoms of human life, and they are denied to no one who earnestly seeks them.

Give yourself permission to say no—and the universe will respond with just one word:

YES!

★ ★ ★

What's the seventh step to overcoming success anorexia?

15

The Seventh Step:
Find Your "Because"

"Find your because" means finding your answer to the question, "What am I really doing here?" Compared to this question, all the others we've asked so far are relatively insignficant.

Finding your **because** comes directly out of finding your no (what we talked about in the last chapter). That's because it's very difficult to find your no if you haven't yet found your because. Conversely, once you've found your because, finding your no will become a no-brainer.

What do I mean by this? Let's look at an obvious example from my own life to illustrate this point.

On the night I discovered success anorexia, I realized that after many years of painful searching, I had finally found my purpose in life. I knew instantly that there were millions of people who were starving themselves of success—doing exactly what I had been doing—but had no idea what was going on. I also knew that I had just been given the information that would help thousands of people overcome this problem.

Do you see how easy that made my life?

What happened as a result of that event was that every other decision I made after that had to be passed through the filter of, "Does this fit into my purpose and the reason I'm here on Earth?"

Therefore, when you have to make a choice about how to spend your time, for example, all you have to do is ask yourself: "Would doing this help me to [x] (whatever your "because" or purpose is)?"

Another way to ask this would be: "Will doing this [whatever I'm contemplating doing] help me fulfill my obligation to the people who need me?"

These are what I call "finding your because" questions, because these types of questions elicit answers that tell you whether what you are thinking about doing is on track with your true purpose or not.

Think about it. If you knew that what you did today was going to affect people—hundreds, even thousands of people down the road—how would that influence how you think about what you're going to do?

Ironically, when we know that our decisions affect other people, it actually eases our decision-making process. I have found, through painful experience, that it is when I feel that "nothing I do matters," my ability to make decisions becomes weak, and I begin to ask myself questions like, "What's the use anyway?"

I firmly believe, and my experience with students around the world has shown, that most people know what to do, that they've already been given all the gifts they could possibly need—but they are refusing to move forward because "the time isn't right" or "I'm too much of this" or "not enough of that" or, if they would really admit it, "I'm scared."

Please, stop doing this to yourself and to the rest of the world. Did you realize that by not expressing your Authentic Self, you are not only not helping others, you are actually hurting them?

Let me explain. I want to close this section of the book by giving you an illustration that has literally worked miracles in my own life and those of my students. If you get nothing else from this book, I would like you to carry this image with you and let it help you let yourself succeed for the rest of your life:

Imagine that you are standing in the world's largest dining room. It is so large that everyone on earth can fit into it. You look around and notice that in front of you is the world's largest buffet table. It stretches far into the distance, from one end of this incomprehensibly large dining room to the other.

On this enormous buffet table is laid out every food in the world, the most succulent, delicious foods you can imagine. You look around again and notice that on every side of this buffet table is every person on earth. This buffet table feeds the world. The line of people stretches as far as you can see.

As you observe this scene, you notice that although everyone is obviously hungry, and some are even starving, noone is eating. The line isn't moving. You look behind you and notice that thousands of people are waiting.

"What are they waiting for?" you ask yourself. And then it hits you.

They are waiting for you.

★   ★   ★

There is a divine order to the universe. Order is heaven's first law.

If you and I do not let ourselves "eat"—that is, to help ourselves to the bounty that life has for us here on earth—we not only hurt ourselves, we hurt others as well.

Remember Jimmy Stewart's character in *It's a Wonderful Life?* Remember what would have happened if this one man had not been born? Do you honestly think that you are any different?

It may be true that in the grand scheme of the life of the universe, our existence on this tiny blue-green planet of ours may not mean much. In fact, it may not mean anything at all.

But it's all we've got.

Will you let yourself eat now?

PART FOUR

Final Thoughts on Success

16

The Three Causes for All Human Failure and How to Avoid Them

Failure. Now there's a yucky word.

I can't think of a feeling I dislike more than the belief that I have failed. Perhaps that's why I've spent so much time studying the causes of success. Ironically, however, the study of one thing inevitably leads to the study of its opposite.

One day while I was eating breakfast, it suddenly dawned on me that of all the seemingly myriad reasons that people fail, they can all be boiled down to just three reasons. I call them the three causes of all human failure.

Here's a brief list of what these causes AREN'T:

- parents

- teachers

- siblings

- the government

- high taxes

- where we grew up

- how we grew up

- if we grew up

- the color of our skin

- our sex

- our age

- our height

- our weight

- ourselves

Please notice again that I said that these DON'T cause human failure. (Hope I stressed that enough.)

I realized that, although we can blame each of these things for our lack of success, there are really only three reasons for all human failure. They are:

- fear

- ignorance

- entropy

Every problem that human beings face—every war, disagreement, lawsuit or argument, everything that bogs us down or ties us up—can be boiled down to one or a combination of these three root causes: fear, ignorance and entropy. Let's examine each one in turn, and then discover how to avoid (or at least overcome) every one of them.

Fear

Fear causes more human failure than any other factor. It may even cause the other two. That's why we'll spend more time discussing fear than the other two causes combined.

What is fear? Fear is simply *the anticipation or the expectation of pain*.

Here's a message that the Negative Reflection doesn't want you to know: We needn't be afraid of fear! Fear is a wonderful paradox. The only way that fear can have any power over us is if we run from, deny or try to avoid it—in other words, if we fear fear.

Fear is simply a message from us to ourselves, which is essentially saying, "Hey! *Whatever you're thinking about doing, I believe that's going to cause me pain. . . . So DON'T DO IT, okay?"*

Fear is nothing to be ashamed of, feel bad about or be afraid of (fear). The Negative Reflection will try to make the victim feel ashamed for even feeling, let alone admitting, that he or she is afraid or feels fear. This seems to be particularly true in men, who have been taught that to feel fear is unmanly, weak or feminine. Of course, many women also feel ashamed of feeling fear.

Members of both sexes need to remember that fear is a natural, normal and healthy reaction to the thought of doing something that we believe might cause an increase in pain to ourselves or to others. Therefore, fear is a simple biological message that nature has put there for a very simple reason: to protect us. It is not something over which we need to feel shame. Paradoxically, just admitting to ourselves or to another person that we fear takes away its potency; fear can only control us when we try to pretend it's not there.

For example, after I discovered success anorexia, I began thinking about appearing on *The Oprah Winfrey Show*, because I greatly admire and respect Ms. Winfrey personally and professionally. She is a brilliant businessperson who has single-handedly inspired Americans to read again. However, appearing on Ms. Winfrey's show would clearly change my life in ways that I couldn't anticipate, because millions of people would instantly learn about success anorexia and how I work with people to help them overcome it.

I began to really ask myself why I felt fear when I thought about getting something that I really wanted, i.e., going on *The Oprah Winfrey Show* and giving millions of people the opportunity to learn how they could significantly improve their lives. I gradually realized that I believed that going on her show would represent the end of my old way of life (i.e., being anonymous) and the beginning of a life that I don't have much experience in (being well-known, perhaps even "famous"). Therefore, I felt fear.

I finally realized that this was simply a message from me to myself, which was saying, *"Hey! I don't know if I want to do this or not! What if doing this will cause me more pain than the pain I'm currently feeling?"* I realized that sentence actually sums up what fear really is: a message from ourselves to ourselves saying, "Hey! What if doing this causes me more pain than the pain I'm currently feeling?"

Fear's job is simply to keep us SAFE. Therefore, when I thought about doing something (i.e., becoming famous) that might cause me more pain than the pain I was currently feeling, what occurred was a message from my body that I understood as fear. (By the way, we're always at a certain level of pain, either high or low; it's not a black-or-white situation, e.g., no pain/all pain.) I felt fear simply because I was thinking about doing something that might cause me more pain than the pain I was currently feeling.

Once I realized what fear really was, I understood how to handle it. I realized that all I really needed was the assurance that I was going to be safe and that everything would be all right. In a very real sense, fear is like your mother. Remember how your mother always warned you: "Don't cross the street without looking. . . . Be sure to put your hat and gloves on when you go outside in the cold. . . . Did you finish your homework? . . ." etc.

Why did your mother do all this fussing over you— because she didn't like you? Of course not. She did it for the exact opposite reason: because she cared about you and wanted you to be safe! A mother's worst fear is that harm will come to her child. That's why she gave you all of these rules by which to live your life. Therefore, I realized that all my fear needed was exactly what a mother needs: the assurance that I'm going to be all right.

And that's how I invented . . .

The Astonishingly Simple Technique for Overcoming Fear

This technique is so astonishingly simple, it may seem almost silly to you. However, I have yet to see a situation in which it does not work, if applied properly. All it takes are three simple steps:

Step 1: When you first feel fear (about doing something), admit it immediately.

The next time you feel fear about doing something, whether it's picking up the phone to call someone, leaving your job or starting a new business, you must first admit that you feel that fear. Right here is where most people let fear get the better of them, because they believe that denying their fear will somehow make it magically go away.

It should come as no surprise to you that precisely the opposite is true. Fear is like a person who's banging at your door, demanding your attention. If you ignore him, he just bangs louder and louder. Then he gets a bunch of his friends to bang on your door. If you try to ignore him long enough, he'll eventually drive a tank through your front door. This "bashing your door in" may come in the form of a car accident, the end of a marriage or a heart attack. (I call this the "two-by-four-in-the-face-from-the-universe" method of getting your attention.)

Therefore, it is absolutely vital that you admit that you feel fear the moment it arises. I am not aware of any other feeling we are so prone to deny than fear (except, perhaps, desire). Please keep in mind that it is not at all necessary for you to tell every single person around you that you feel fear. The only person you really need to admit it to is yourself. However, it is perfectly acceptable and even recommended for you to tell people whom you can trust about your fear.

Step 2: Put a picture and a face to your fear.

In other words, imagine exactly what your fear looks like.

Does your fear look like a big, green, scaly monster? A tiny little man? An orangutan? Your mother? Your father? Your brother or sister?

The point is, your fear came from somewhere. You did not just make it up. Every fear that we have is perfectly justifiable and has its basis in reality, just like every other emotion we feel. The challenge is that we tend to stay stuck in our fear, for the very reasons that I am explaining here. Therefore, in order to make our fear more real, I am suggesting that you find out what it looks like. (Stay with me on this one.) I know this sounds counterintuitive, because we have been trained to deny and run from fear. All you need to ask yourself is, "Is what I'm currently doing working?" You know as well as I do that if you want to keep getting what you're getting, just keep doing what you're doing.

I strongly suggest that you draw a color picture of what your fear looks like. (I have a picture called "Noah Shaking Hands with His Fear" in which I drew fear as this goofy, green dinosaur.) You might also put yourself in the picture as you relate to your fear. (In the picture I just mentioned, I drew myself with really long hair, like I always wanted. Why not?) Okay, you've put a face to your fear. Now you're ready for:

Step 3: Thank your fear for doing such a great job of protecting you.

This is the one that will really blow you away.

Now that you've admitted that you feel fear, and know what your fear looks like, it's time to thank it for doing such a great job of taking care of you. "What?!" you may be thinking. "Fear is the thing that's kept me from what I wanted to do! Fear is the reason I'm stuck in this lousy situation! And you want me to thank it for doing a great job of taking care of me?"

You got it.

Fear is like the brakes of our car. It might be fun to drive wherever we wanted to go without needing to stop, but the rules of the road and the facts of life dictate that we do need to slow down, even stop (sometimes very quickly) every once in a while. We run into problems, however, if we're constantly driving around with one foot on the brake and one foot on the gas.

The way to take your foot off the brake is to acknowledge that fear has actually done a pretty great job of protecting you from what you thought would cause you pain. For example, I believed that if I got involved with a woman I liked, she would leave me. Therefore, whenever I saw an attractive woman, I naturally felt fear. It took me years to discover why I felt fear when I met a beautiful, available woman to whom I was attracted.

It wasn't exactly pleasant to have to go through all those years of torture to figure out what I just told you. However, once I did, I had to finally admit that my fear had done a pretty amazing job of protecting me from what I believed was a situation in which I could be harmed: in other words, someone whom I loved leaving me.

Therefore, the trick to overcoming fear is to simply acknowledge that it has done a great job of protecting you from what you believe will cause you harm. To return to a previous analogy, when the little guy starts banging on the door, don't wait for him to get all his friends and bash in your front door with a tank. Open the door and invite him in for tea. You will be amazed by how quickly this tiger becomes a pussycat, when you simply listen to what he's saying and thank him for his input.

When you invite your fear in for tea, simply say to it (out loud, on paper or just in your mind) something like this:

"Oh, hi! It's you, Fear. I'm so glad you're here! Thank you so much for wanting to protect me and keep me safe from harm. You are doing such a great job, you're trying to keep me safe from things that haven't even happened yet!

"So," you can continue, "what you're really asking me,

Fear, is, 'Will doing what I'm thinking about doing cause me more pain than the pain I'm currently feeling?' Well, Fear, I have to admit to you, I honestly don't know if doing this (whatever it is) will cause me more pain than the pain I'm currently feeling.

"But you know what, Fear?" you can say. "I really need to find out for myself. I have a lot of friends who are going to be here to help me through whatever pain will be there. So, thanks again for your input. See you later!"

That, as they say, is that.

You have just taken away ALL of Fear's power—by simply acknowledging that it's there, and thanking it for trying to protect you from things that haven't even happened yet. You might also think of Fear as a little child tugging at your pants leg to get your attention. If you try to ignore the child, he or she only becomes more insistent. When you use the astonishingly simple technique just described, it's like giving a piece of candy to a little child.

The next time you feel that old feeling you know as fear, follow the above steps. I like to picture me and my fear sitting down to a cup of tea. (You don't have to be crazy to do this work, but it does help.) Tell your fear what you are thinking of doing. For example, if you are considering:

- going on *The Oprah Winfrey Show;*

- being more successful than you are now;

- speaking in front of a group of people;
- calling someone you want to go out with;
- calling someone you don't know;
- going on a job interview;
- trying anything new;

realize that it is perfectly reasonable for you to feel fear, because you are trying something new. It stands to reason that trying something new might cause you more pain than the pain you are currently feeling. Therefore, doesn't it make sense that you would get a message from yourself saying: "Hey! I don't know if I want to do this or not! What if doing this causes me more pain than the pain I'm currently feeling?"

Therefore, all you need to do is say to your fear, "Oh, hi, Fear, how are you? Thank you for trying to protect me from harm; I really appreciate it. By the way, you're right: doing this might cause me more pain than the pain I'm currently feeling. Then again, it might mean that I feel less pain than I'm currently feeling. How about we find out together?"

In this way, you can turn your fear from your worst enemy into one of your closest friends, and use it as nature intended—our greatest internal mechanism for keeping us from harm. (For a further discussion of how you can convert fear from an enemy into a friend, please read Gavin De Becker's superb book, *The Gift of Fear*.)

Ignorance

The word *ignorance* comes from the Latin word meaning "we do not know." It means "being unaware or uninformed." Ignorance in this sense doesn't mean being uneducated. The ignorance that causes failure is "that which we believe or think is so, that is not so." Put another way, ignorance represents what we believe about ourselves, other people and the universe that is not supported by facts or by truth. (As Will Rogers once said, "It ain't what a man knows that gets him in trouble. It's what he knows that ain't so.")

We all believe something about everything and everybody in the universe. For example, if I believe that trees are bad, I will act as though this belief were true. Just because I believe it to be true doesn't mean that it *is* true. However, my actions will be such that I believe that it's true—and until and unless I change my mind about trees, no amount of facts will change my mind. (As someone once put it, "Don't confuse me with the facts.")

Similarly, when a person's core beliefs come from the Negative Reflection, as in the case of the success anorexic, what the person believes about herself or himself will have no basis in reality or truth at all (e.g., I'm no good; Everyone hates me; I should just die; etc.). Until and unless these individuals learn that they are NOT, in fact, no good; that everyone does NOT hate them; and that they should NOT just die, they will not be able to fully accept or enjoy their own success.

In this way, ignorance of who they are, and a misunderstanding of their relationship to the universe, causes these individuals to refuse to succeed. Ignorance is just like fear in this sense: It can only cause failure when we refuse to acknowledge it. We can make ignorance one of our greatest teachers by simply acknowledging that we don't know everything.

Why It's So Hard to Ask for Help

Many people would almost (or literally) rather die than ask for help. Most of us were not taught how to ask for help in school or in our families; indeed, in many cases, we were taught to *not* ask for help. Do any of the following messages sound familiar to you?

"Don't be so selfish."

"Don't talk back to your elders."

"Don't you know that by now?"

"Children should be seen and not heard."

"Because I'm your mother, that's why."

Anyone want to ask for help now? Didn't think so.

We overcome ignorance first by acknowledging that it's there—that is, admitting to ourselves and others that there is something we don't know. Second, we realize that there is someone, somewhere, who knows what we need to know. Third, we ask for the help we need by giving the other person what he or she really wants first.

What Every Human Being Really Wants and How to Get It

Here is everything you will ever need to know about everyone you will ever meet for the rest of your life: *Every human being really wants only three things: approval, appreciation and attention.* Of course, every individual wants these in different amounts, and some need much, much more of these three things than others. However, you will never meet the person who doesn't want approval, who doesn't want to be appreciated or who doesn't want some kind of positive attention. (This does not mean, by the way, that every person you meet will be comfortable receiving these things.)

Did you notice something amazing about what every human being really wants? They're all free! Not one of them costs you a dime. Therefore, all you have to do to get everything you want for the rest of your life is to give everyone you meet what they really want: approval, appreciation and attention. Can you imagine the world we'd live in if we all started doing this?

"How am I supposed to do this?" you might ask. Most self-help books say that you have to give them to yourself before you can give them to anyone else. Frankly, however, I disagree. It's almost always easier to give approval, appreciation and attention to other people than it is to give them to yourself. Therefore, instead of sitting around trying to love yourself, give love to those around you. You will find that this simple act will increase your own sense of self-esteem, because, as Ralph Waldo Emerson said, "It is impossible to give love to someone else without some of it getting on you."

Call your best friend and tell him or her how grateful you are that he or she is in your life. Call each of your children and thank them for doing such a good job of raising you. Call your son or daughter and tell them how proud you are of them, not for what they do, but for the persons they are. One caveat: Only do this if you can say these things and mean them. Your words do not have to come out perfectly. Your message will get through loud and clear.

Once you have given other people what they really want, it becomes increasingly easy to ask for the help we need. It is as though each of us has an internal help sensor that detects when someone needs our help. The challenge is that we often try to deny our own need for help, thereby short-circuiting other people's sensors.

We can overcome this habit of denying our need for help by simply acknowledging that we are human and finite, and do not know everything. It is neither possible nor necessary for any one person to know all the ways to live a healthy or successful life. Therefore, the way to overcome ignorance is to simply acknowledge its presence, admit the gaps in our knowledge and ask for the help we need. (Easier said than done? You bet it is.)

Entropy

The third cause for human failure, **entropy,** is the only one that's a natural principle—that is, a law that appears in nature as well as in human behavior. The law of entropy states that all things tend to decay and become disordered over time. (Just think of your car, your desk or your closet.)

The word *entropy* comes from the Greek word meaning "in transformation." In its essential sense, this law means that all things are always changing. However, the nature of change is such that things always seem to move toward a more chaotic or disorganized state! One of the most fascinating parts of entropy is that human beings are the only creatures on earth who have the capability to overcome entropy, because we're the only creatures who have a say in who we are, who we want to be and where we want to go.

How do we overcome entropy? All you have to do is realize that entropy will always win in the end. "What?!" (Stay with me on this one.)

Realizing the truth about entropy doesn't make sense if you look at it in the limited sense that most people do. Most people try to fight change with everything they've got. They resist, they struggle, they put up fights, they demand that life show up the way they want it to—and wonder why they're exhausted by two o'clock every day.

The only constant of life is change. Change means something different from what has happened in the past. The reason people fight and resist change so much is actually fear of change, fear of the unknown, fear of having or doing or getting something different.

However, for many people, what really scares them is the fear that nothing will change and that everything will stay the same! Success anorexics, in particular, fear that the constant barrage from the Negative Reflection will never go away and that they'll never be free.

Amazingly, when students learn that life is change, they tend to relax and become more at ease. They realize that what they were fighting was not just themselves, but the very nature of life itself. When they are shown that they are not responsible for fixing either themselves or life itself, it may be the first time they have ever heard that information. It may take several weeks or months of repetition, but gradually my students begin to believe it.

We have a statement at The Success Clinic: "The world will just have to take care of itself." Lest it sound to the reader that we're creating a bunch of selfish people, please remember that the person who develops success anorexia has felt responsible for the entire world. This could hardly be the behavior of a selfish person.

Frankly, students needs to be reminded (or told for the first time) that saving the world is not their job at all. It's entirely appropriate that we tell our students that the world will just have to take care of itself. We overcome entropy by acknowledging that it will always win in the end, but that we can win in little ways while we're still alive.

That is why we exercise, eat properly, breathe deeply, read, write and listen to other people's experiences. Otherwise, entropy will overtake our bodies (being out of shape), our minds (not wanting to learn) and our spirits (not asking the important questions of life). That's how you can make entropy into a good friend—by remembering that it will always win in the end, and to take steps to defeat it, just a little bit, every day.

★ ★ ★

Isn't it amazing that the only way to avoid and overcome the three causes for all human failure is to make friends with them? In other words:

We humans will always fear something; but we needn't fear fear.

We humans will always be ignorant about something; but we can find what we need to know, by giving others what they really want first.

And even though entropy will win in the end, we can win today by acknowledging entropy's presence, and taking steps to counteract it (exercising our minds, bodies and spirits).

Even though we won't do this perfectly, isn't it great to know how to overcome the causes for all human failure?

★ ★ ★

What are three simple facts about success that almost everyone ignores?

17

Three Simple Facts About Success That Almost Everyone Ignores

You would think when we talk about something that has been studied, dissected and desired as much as "success," that there would be almost universal agreement about what it is and how to get it. Amazingly, however, there remains an air of mystery, suspense and confusion around this thing we call "success."

The reason for this is both simple and complex: Many of us simply do not feel successful. However (and this is what causes the mystery and suspense), very few people will ever admit, except in their most intimate moments, that they do not feel successful. Most of us defend our actions and our opinions to the death—

even though they may be the very things that have stopped us from getting what we want!

In this chapter, we're going to examine three simple facts about success that almost everyone ignores—and, in fact, that few people will even admit are true. We're going to simultaneously bust what I call the top three "Success Myths"—that is, beliefs about success that many people think are true but that are not substantiated by facts. (We could examine ten or twenty-five or one hundred myths about success, but I think you'll find that these three will cover most of the mystery, suspense and confusion behind this thing we call "success.")

Before we get to these Success Myths and their related Success Facts, let's remember what a fact is. A *fact* is something that can be objectively verified; something with real, demonstrable existence. When we speak about facts, it's important to remember what we're NOT speaking about:

We're not talking about opinions. The word *opinion* comes from a Latin word meaning "to suppose," and is "a belief or idea held with confidence but not sustantiated by direct proof or knowledge." For example, for years I held the opinion that "I shouldn't want (to succeed) *too* much." The reason I held this opinion was that it was clearly supported by my experience. Remember when I called my father and asked him if it would be okay with him if I became more successful than he was? The reason

I felt I needed to do that was because I honestly didn't know if it was okay with him if I became very successful. (Yes, I knew that I could become, perhaps, moderately successful, but anything more than that . . . well, I just didn't know if that would be okay.)

Thankfully, my dad encouraged me to be as successful as I wanted to be. This is exactly how most of our opinions are formed—by our experience. As Napoleon Hill wrote in *Think and Grow Rich*, however, the problem is not that we don't know enough, but that our experience is often faulty. In other words, my opinion that it was not okay for me to become very successful was not a fact at all, even though it was supported by my experience (what I saw and felt). Therefore, just because we hold an opinion that something is true, does not make it a fact.

When we talk about facts, we're also not talking about *beliefs*. A belief is similar to an opinion, in that it is usually based upon our experience. For example, many years ago, most human beings believed that the earth was flat and that the sun revolved around it. This belief was based upon our observations of natural phenomena through the measuring instruments that were available to us at the time—namely, our eyes. However, when human beings created instruments that could measure the universe with greater accuracy than just our physical senses could (i.e., telescopes and the ability to use advanced mathematics), these beliefs were shown to be false (incompatible with demonstrable data or facts).

When we speak of facts, therefore, we are talking about things (phenomena, data, observable events) that can be shown to be objectively true, accurate or correct. The trick to all of this lies in just one word: objective. Frankly, it is simply impossible for you or I to be objective about anything.

Why? Because the word *objective* means "uninfluenced by emotion, surmise or personal opinion." In other words, it means "having no point of view." That's kind of like saying, "Not being human." If we are looking at something, we must have a perspective or "point" that we are "viewing" it from.

The point is, we do not have to agree with facts for them to be true, accurate or correct. In fact, much of what creates human misery (and much of the cause of human failure) is the ignorance, misuse, miscommunication or misunderstanding of facts.

Therefore, when we speak of three simple facts about success that almost everyone ignores, I don't believe that presenting these facts is going to in any way change anyone's mind about them. I expect that many people will vehemently disagree with the statements below. That's fine; but the thing about facts is that they just sit there. They simply ARE. We can fight, ignore, be unaware of and try to make them change, all we want.

But all of our fighting, ignoring and arguing won't make the Sun go around the Earth.

Therefore, no matter what our opinions, experiences or beliefs are, they aren't going to change these three simple facts about success that almost everyone ignores:

Fact #1: It's harder to fail than to succeed.

Fact #2: Success is natural. Life really wants and actually needs us to succeed.

Fact #3: Success means asking the right questions and refusing to ask the wrong ones.

If these are truly facts, they must be able to be objectively verified. Knowing that, again, true objectivity is impossible (because true objectivity would mean "having no point of view"—and since we're examining these things, we must have a point of view to do so, right?), let's examine these facts with as much objectivity as we can muster. (Note: I will list the three Success Myths alongside the three Success Facts to ease our discussion.)

Success Myth #1: Success is hard.

Success Fact #1: It is harder to fail than to succeed.

I bet that one got you up out of your chair!

"What do you mean, it's harder to fail than to succeed? I've been working my tail off for umpteen years, and I'm still not where I want to be in life! Listen, buddy, let me tell you: Success is hard!"

See? Told you objectivity was difficult.

Okay. If the statement "It is harder to fail than to succeed" is a fact, it must be able to be proven. Let's see if we can do this.

First of all, it's important to note that when I speak of success, I am not simply talking about the first thing that pops into most people's heads when we say the word "success"—namely, "money." I am not going to sit here and tell you that you don't have to work hard to make a lot of money. Most of us do have to do quite a number of things quite well for quite a long time before we get to the place we would call "having a lot of money."

However (and this is the key), having a lot of money is never the direct result of hard work. In fact, it takes much more work and effort to keep money (and success) away from us than to let it in.

Let me give you an example. My father is the hardest-working person I've ever met. Next to my father, Michelangelo was a slacker. My father is a writer, a painter, a musician, a graphic artist, a design engineer, an actor, a director and a producer—and did all this while he had three very lively children and a wife to take care of.

My father opened an advertising agency in which he worked an average of eighty to one hundred hours per week. I remember going to his office on Main Street in Kennebunk, Maine, when I was a boy. There were four people working there, including my mother, and they always seemed busy and looked like they were designing or creating something really neat. I didn't know what it all meant, but they were busy so I thought everything was going well.

The problem was my father got into business with a rather unscrupulous fellow who decided he wanted to take more than his share of the business. My father's attitude at the time, he told me years later, was, "I'll take care of the creative part and you [the other fellow] take care of the business part." Well, the other fellow took care of the business part all right—enough so that after years of one-hundred-hour weeks and missing most of his children's childhoods, my family was broke, we couldn't pay our mortgage and we lost our house.

Now, my father's story may not be typcial of what happens in business, although it is certainly not uncommon. The point is that all of my father's hard work did not produce either financial or emotional success, because he simply did not take the time nor did he have the interest to understand how money and human beings really operate.

Years later, my father told me that he used to believe that if he were just a "nice guy" that people would want to pay him lots of money for his services. It should come as no surprise to you that, even though my father was and is an incredibly gifted artist, people didn't exactly go out of their way to pay him lots of money.

My father also told me, after he read the first edition of the book you are holding, "Noah, I felt like I was reading my autobiography. I wish you had written this twenty years ago." (Well, gee, I would have loved to, but I was only twelve at the time . . .)

The point is, it is much harder to fail than to succeed for one very simple reason: Life is set up so that it is actually impossible to fail. We always succeed in whatever we choose. That statement may sound strange or unbelievable to you. But here are the facts:

The universe is set in motion by our thoughts, words and actions. What we think, say (believe) and do sets into motion of string of events that produce the results we get in our lives. Therefore, if you think to yourself, "I'll never be successful," the universe says, "Okay." And you succeed at not succeeding.

If you say to yourself, "I will be successful," the universe says, "Okay." And you do the things and make the choices that produce success in your life. The universe is simply a perfect mirror of our thoughts, words and actions. It is impossible for us to fail because we always create precisely and exactly what we choose.

The key to understanding this is that a) many of us say and do things that we do not necessarily believe (in), and b) we do not always consciously choose what we want. Instead, many of us unconsciously choose what we do NOT want. This sets up a dichotomy in the universe which the universe still supports. If we are doing this, we are literally moving at cross-purposes—trying hard to achieve success on one hand, unconsciously pushing it away with the other. The universe has no choice but to always support our thoughts, words and actions, and so, in this case, we would get close to success, only to have it torn from our grasp.

We may not like it or be able to admit it, but the fact remains that the universe supports whatever we repeatedly think, say and do. Recognizing this truth, some of the best works of traditional success literature have advocated the use of "affirmations" to change our thoughts, words and actions from self-defeating to self-supporting. In just a few moments, however, I am going to show you something that may blow you away: I am going to show you why affirmations don't really work the way they are supposed to.

In order to do that, I am going to share with you a process that I discovered almost by accident—a way to get whatever you want in life by using a method that's so incredibly simple, you are already doing it and don't even know it.

But before I do that, let's look at the second of our Success Myths and Success Facts:

Success Myth #2: Life is against us and we've got to struggle and suffer to get ahead.

Success Fact #2: Success is natural, because life really wants and actually needs us to succeed.

To prove this, let's again turn to the facts (remember, we're not concerned with opinions or beliefs here; only facts):

Human beings are an expression of life itself. This is evidenced by the fact that life exists, and nothing can exist outside of life itself. If we are alive, therefore, we must be an expression of life itself.

Life expresses in the universe through the use and application of law. In other words, there is no effect in the universe without an accompanying cause. This law is often called the law of cause and effect or, as Emerson called it, the law of laws. The most common expression of this law is: You reap what you sow ("as ye sow, so shall ye reap").

The purpose of life is to express itself. Life is always for expansion and fuller expression of itself. Therefore, since we human beings manifest or express life itself, and the purpose of life is for expansion and fuller expression, life must want and actually need us to succeed. Life cannot possibly be against itself, for this would break its own law.

When you or I do this thing we call "succeed," then, what you are really doing is expressing more of Who You

Really Are, because you and I are an expression of life itself, whose purpose is to express itself. When you succeed, therefore, what you are really doing is *giving other people the courage to be and express Who They Really Are*.

Don't you think that life would want you to do more of that?

Want proof? Here's a question for you: have you ever heard a story of someone who started out with nothing, overcame tremendous odds, persevered and then succeeded beyond their wildest dreams? What was the effect of their story on you? Didn't their story inspire you?

The word *inspire* literally means "to breathe in." Therefore, when we are "inspired" by someone or something, what really happens is that we are given the courage to breathe, to be and to express more of Who We Really Are.

Doesn't it make sense that life would want and actually need more of that? If the purpose of life is to be expressed, don't you think that life wants you to succeed (whatever "success" means to you)—in order that life itself may be expressed?

The purpose of a seed is to grow. The purpose of nature is to support the growth of all seeds into whatever they grow into. And the purpose of life is to be and to express more of itself than has ever been or expressed before.

By the way, every piece of spiritual, religious or sacred literature, as well as every work of science, art and philosophy, is simply an expression of this desire of life to be and to express itself. It seems that we humans get to explore and express more of life than any other creature on earth. (I often say that when you come to earth as a human being, you arrive in your "explore the universe" body.)

Which brings us to the biggest Success Myth, and the most overlooked yet simplest Success Fact of all:

Success Myth #3: Success means having all the answers.

Success Fact #3: Success means asking the right questions and refusing to ask the wrong ones.

Suppose I were to ask you to list everything that's wrong with, lacking in or not good enough about you. If you're like most people, you could go on for days. Now suppose I asked you to tell me everything that's great, good, superb, terrific and wonderful about you. Can you name ten things that are great about you? Most people have a hard time coming up with two.

Why are we so quick to point out our weaknesses and shortcomings, yet find it nearly impossible to name our strengths, our assets and what's simply outstanding about ourselves?

To answer this question, let's look at our training as children. Most of us were not very subtly taught that it was wrong to be conceited. Most of us heard messages from well-meaning parents and elders that went something like this: "Don't be conceited. . . . No one will like you if you talk about yourself too much. . . . Who do you think you are? . . . Don't get too big for your britches. . . . Nobody likes a show-off. . . . Children should be seen and not heard. . . ."

It's clear that in most cases, our elders really wanted the best for us and actually (believe it or not) wanted us to be happy. Unfortunately, most of them were completely unaware of the power that their words had to shape our lives. It's obvious that as children we want to please our parents. Therefore, when we received from our parents messages like those listed above, we naturally tried to stop saying good things about ourselves. The problem is that we got *too* good at it.

That's why so many of us as adults can't think good thoughts about ourselves or speak well of ourselves. We did such a good job of not thinking well of ourselves that we're hard-pressed to find anything that's right about ourselves any more.

This is also the source of the Negative Reflection: the attempt of the person (our Authentic Self) to make sense of a world that makes no sense at all. For example, the child sees and knows that there is a problem, an unhappiness or something that needs to be "fixed" in the family. Naturally, she tries to fix it. When she finds that

her efforts not only don't fix the problem, but that others don't even seem to be aware that there is a problem,
her thinking goes something like this: "If I were only
good enough, I would be able to fix this problem and
make everyone happy." However, since she also notices
that the "problem" does not seem to go away, but often
gets worse, the only possible conclusion that she could
come to is, "I must not be good enough." Therefore, the
Negative Reflection is actually a logical response to what
the child senses from his or her environment—a way to
make sense of the childs nonsensical world.

Luckily for the victims, the Negative Reflection and the
success anorexic's distorted self-image, are not based upon
facts at all, but upon their beliefs—beliefs that made sense
for the child, but have no place in the adult world. That is
precisely how we overcome and reverse this condition.

For example, the Negative Reflection continually
bombards its victims with questions like, "How could you
be so selfish? . . . Who do you think you are? . . . Why
aren't you any better than you are? . . ." etc. But here is a
simple, commonly ignored fact about success that may
just change your life forever:

*When you change the questions you ask yourself, you
must get different answers.*

When you get different answers, you get a different life.

A New Discovery: The Power of Afformations

One night in the spring of 1997, I was listening to an audiotape program of a speaker who was saying that the human mind operates using questions. He stated that the process of thinking is really nothing more than the asking and answering of questions.

For example, suppose I asked you, "Why is the sky blue?" What would happen? What would happen is that your brain would say, "The sky is blue because . . ." and then search its "database" for the answer to the question. Even if you didn't know the answer, your brain would still try to look for an answer. (In this instance, your brain would come back with the response, "I don't know" or, in computer lingo, "File not found.")

Please notice, however, that the one thing your brain can't do is NOT try to find the answer to the question that is presented to it. That is, once you ask the human brain/yourself/the universe a question, you can't NOT try to find the answer to it. (This doesn't necessarily mean that you will find or know the answer yet; it simply means that you can't NOT try to find an answer when you sincerely ask your mind the question.)

As I was listening to the speaker talk about how the mind operates using questions, I started thinking about a technique that I'm sure you're familiar with: the process of using affirmations. The reason I'm sure you've heard of them is because the benefits of using of affirmations has been stated in nearly every work of traditional success literature. An affirmation is a positive statement intended to create the things that we want in our lives by saying, stating, thinking or writing them repeatedly.

I started to think about the use of affirmations as I thought about how the brain really operates. At the risk of stepping on a few toes here, here's what I realized: using affirmations doesn't really work correctly.

"What do you mean?" I heard some of you say. "Isn't traditional success literature built upon the use of positive statements intended to produce a result in our lives?" It sure is.

Let's return to the facts to examine this argument. The human brain operates by the simple process of asking and answering questions. (Did you notice what your mind is doing right now? Isn't it asking itself a question like, "Are you sure that's right?" "Is that what I'm really doing?" And what are those? Questions!) Frankly, it's simply impossible for the human brain to NOT be engaged in the process of asking and attempting to answer questions.

After I heard this fact about the human mind—that questions are literally the human brain's operating system—I asked myself a very simple question (see?):

"If the human brain is always engaged in the process of asking and attempting to answer questions, and the brain literally can't NOT try to find an answer that is put to it, why are we going around using empowering statements to try and improve our lives . . .

". . . instead of using empowering questions?"

And you know what? I could not find a satisfactory answer to that question.

Without even meaning to—and solely through the process of asking the questions I have just described to you—I (almost accidentally) invented something completely new in the study of success. It is called the use of afformations.

What is an afformation? And how is it different from an affirmation?

Good question.

An afformation is an empowering question to which the human brain must try to find an answer. After I discovered and named afformations, I realized why affirmations don't really work correctly. You see, the brain is always asking and answering questions, right? (Another question.) That means that you or I can make all the positive statements (affirmations) we want; but if we haven't changed the questions we are asking ourselves, our statements will have no effect whatsoever.

For example, you could be going around saying, "I'm happy, healthy and wealthy." However, inside you may be asking yourself, "Where is it? How come I'm so unhappy? Why am I still broke? Why can't I do anything right?" In other words, your affirmative statement will not change your life in the least if you continue to ask yourself lousy questions.

Can't you corroborate this with your own experience? Haven't you tried to use affirmations—written and spoken positive statements intended to elicit a response from the universe—and ended up frustrated and even angry because the statements didn't really come true?

The fault was not yours. The fault was in the technique that you used. And even that wasn't your fault, because no one had ever bothered to mention to you before, that using statements is not nearly as effective as asking empowering questions.

The bottom line is that questions asked *of* the mind are far more powerful than statements that are tacked *onto* the mind. I reasoned, therefore: why not just bypass the statements altogether and go right to the question— since that's what your brain is already doing anyway?

After I created this technique, I coined the word afformation to describe it. Now, I did not just pull this word out of my alphabet soup. I created the word afformation from the Latin word *formare*, which means "to create a shape or give form to." (By the way, the word affirmation comes from the Latin word *firmare* meaning "to make firm." But what if we're "making something firm" in the wrong "shape or form"?)

In case you think this is the nuttiest thing you've ever

heard, let me remind you that when we discover a new way of looking at something, we need to create a new way of talking about it. Not long ago, the words "Internet," "software," and "hard drive" did not even exist. These new words, and scores of others, were developed to describe new ways of doing useful things. Why must the study of success—surely a useful practice—be any different?

In case you still doubt the veracity of this technique, let me offer one final fact: you are already using afformations all the time anyway. In fact, it is actually impossible for you to NOT be using afformations.

Think about it. What is the question: "Why are you so stupid?" or, "How could you be so selfish?" or, "Why doesn't anyone want me around?" or, "Why was I born?" or, "Why don't you just die?" Aren't these simply negative afformations? They are actually the Negative Reflection's way of "giving shape" to itself inside your mind. Therefore, please understand that you and I and every other human being are already using afformations all the time anyway (most of them negative). However, we are completely unaware of this fact nearly 100 percent of the time, and most of us don't realize that the questions we consistently ask ourselves are actually producing what we call "our life."

That's why afformations are so much more powerful and so much more effective than affirmations. In fact, I truly believe that the only time an affirmation (a statement) works at all is when it creates a corresponding affromation (a question) inside the head of the user. In other words, the only time the statement "I'm happy, healthy and wealthy" can produce any changes in your life is when you begin to ask yourself the questions, "Why am I happy? Why am I healthy? Why am I wealthy?"

Why waste all that time, effort, and energy using statements (that often don't work anyway), when your brain has to convert them to questions in order to make any difference in your life? Why not simply ask better questions, and let your brain do what it's already doing (and what it can't NOT do)?

You may want to go back and read this section again. If the process of asking empowering questions seems "too easy" or "too simple," you're right on track. Afformations are indeed incredibly easy and astonishingly simple, precisely because your brain is already using them. However, most of us unconsciously use negative afformations instead of consciously using positive ones.

When you use afformations consciously and positively (reflecting what you want in your life instead of what you don't want), you will not have to wait long to see results (like you do with affirmations), because afformations are already creating your life anyway!

Again, the only time an affirmation will "stick" is when you change the corresponding and underlying question (afformation) associated with it. I am suggesting that you bypass the statement and go right to the question. Here are some more sample afformations to help you get started:

- Why am I so beautiful?

- Why am I so smart?

- Why do I always say and do the right thing?

- How did I get to be so attractive?

- Why am I so attractive?

- Why do so many beautiful, delightful people love me so much?

- Why am I so safe?

- Why am I so taken care of?

- Why do so many people appreciate and value me and what I do for them?

- Why am I so wonderful?

- Why do I always get what I really need at exactly the right time for me?

I have no doubt that these will sound pretty silly to you the first few times you use them. You didn't enter the Indy 500 the first time you got in a car, either.

You may have noticed that many of the examples of

afformations I've given you begin with the word "why." Why do you think this is? Remember in chapter 4 when we realized that 90 percent of human motivation comes from why-to's and only 10 percent comes from our how-to's? This principle is directly applied when we use positive afformations.

Since your brain has to try to find an answer to any question you persistently ask it, when you keep asking yourself "Why?" you will not only find answers, you will be tapping into the 90 percent of you that makes you function. This brings up a good point: The point of asking afformations is NOT to find the answers to your questions! After you ask an afformation, you do not have to sit there and try to answer the question.

Instead, what's likely to happen is that you will simply start to notice that you feel differently when you ask it. Remember, your brain is like a computer. When you ask a computer to do something (by giving it a command), it can't say to you, "Sorry, I don't feel like doing that right now." It has no choice but to try and fulfill your command.

Once you put the question in motion, it's irrevocable. Irreversible. A done deal. That's why you don't need to worry about finding all, or even any, of the answers to your questions. Your brain must try to answer them. Here's what will begin to happen once you begin to replace negative afformations with positive ones:

You will start to feel better. Why? Because you asked, "Why do I feel better?"

You will gain confidence. Why? Because you asked, "Why am I so confident?"

You will begin to realize that all of those self-defeating images and messages you've believed about yourself for so long were wrong. Why? Because you asked, "Why am I so wonderful, awesome, and terrific?"

You'll start to marvel at yourself. Why? Because you asked, "Why am I enough?"

Don't worry about asking perfect afformations. All you ever need to do for the rest of your life is ask yourself, "What would be a great question to ask myself right now?", and let your brain do the work by itself. (That's what it can't not do anyway.)

The invention and use of afformations represents a significant breakthrough in the study of success. In fact, more people have told me that the use of afformations has changed their lives than any other factor in this book. Remember, however, that you're already using afformations anyway, although you may be using them unconsciously. Now that you have read what you and your brain are doing, it is impossible for you to NOT be aware of it any more. (As Emerson said, "A mind once stretched cannot resume its former shape.") Why not use afformations consciously, to create the life you've always wanted?

By the way, (and here's that sentence that gave me so much trouble; I have re-written it so many times that I can't even remember what it says now):

"Why am I alive?"

★ ★ ★

The most important question contained in this book can be found by turning the page.

18

What Is Success?

This may seem like a funny place to ask this question. After all, we've just spent an entire book examining why people do and do not achieve success, why we fear and desire success, and why life really wants and actually needs us to have and enjoy our own success.

Have you ever noticed how, with all of the books and programs out there that talk about success, few of them ever tell you what success actually is?

Frankly, after studying literally hundreds of books, articles and other materials about success, I don't recall any of them ever giving a definition of what success actually is. Yes, they talked about what it meant to succeed, and that success is more than money, wealth and material things, and all of that—but I don't remember any of them giving a precise definition of what success actually *is*, let alone why life wants us to have it.

What, then, is success? I am asked that question more than any other. Here is the answer:

The word *success* comes from the Latin word meaning "to go after" (*sub-*, after + *cedere*, to go). (Isn't it fascinating that the very thing that most of us chase after in life is success, and that the word itself comes from the word meaning "to go after"?) Success simply means "the gaining of something desired, planned or attempted."

This brings up another fascinating aspect of the word *success*—or, more accurately, the word *succeed*. *Succeed* means "to follow next after in time or succession; to replace another in an office or position." An example of this is "to succeed to the throne."

Let's stop a moment and consider that definition in terms of what success actually is. Think about all of the success stories you've ever heard in your life. Did you realize that every success story in history is really a *replacement story?*

What I mean by that is success is literally the process of replacing something (e.g., an activity or a product) with something better, something that produces a more beneficial outcome for a set of human beings or for humanity as a whole. For example:

Galileo replaced the human eye with the telescope.

Albert Einstein replaced the laws of Newton with the understanding of the atom.

Henry Ford replaced the single-line production system with the mass-production process.

Thomas Edison replaced the oil lamp with the incandescent lightbulb.

Every success story you could name is really the story of a person who replaced something with something else, something that served human beings better. The greater the number of people who liked the new thing better than the old thing that it replaced, the more successful the success story. Sheds a different light on the subject of "success" than we're used to, doesn't it?

To use an analogy: if you want to go somewhere in your car, you don't just get in, turn the thing on, step on the gas and let it go wherever it wants to go. You steer the vehicle to where you want it to go. That's your job. The vehicle's job is to get you there faster than you could get there using your own power of locomotion (that's why we like our cars so much).

In a similar manner, when you're headed for success, it would make your job a whole lot easier if you knew where you were going before you got in your vehicle. To help make your job easier, may I present a definition of success that you can use as both your vehicle and your destination?

When we take into account all that has been presented in this book, we can see that success is simply *the process* of asking better questions. Amazingly, success is also the *result* of asking better questions.

More opportunities for success exist today than at any other time in history. However, if we're asking ourselves and others lousy questions, those opportunities don't exist at all. Please notice: I did not say that success means that you have to find all the right answers. It is not your job or mine to know all—or even any—of the right answers.

If You Really Want to Succeed, Do This

Ask better questions.

Ask the questions that people really want and need answered.

Ask questions that no one's yet dared to ask.

Ask questions that make you question reality once in a while.

Ask better questions . . .

Keep asking . . .

and let life take care of the rest.

★ ★ ★

What is success?

Success, dear reader, is to ask better questions . . .

and let life give you every answer you can dream of.

★ ★ ★

19

Where to Find the
Help You Need

Now that you understand the problem of success anorexia, where can you find more help to overcome this condition?

Medical and Health Professionals

Some medical and health professionals are trained to work with eating disorders such as anorexia and bulimia. Obviously, the needs of the person with a success disorder will be somewhat different, though the processes to overcome them may be similar.

Most medical practitioners are very caring individuals who really want to help people.

It's important that you know both the strengths and the limitations of standard health practices, and the people who practice them, and take the appropriate steps that are right for you.

Traditional Success Literature

Yes, these are the ones you've been reading and listening to all your life, and yes, the ones that have (unwittingly) contributed to the problem of success anorexia. Why, then, am I recommending them?

I am recommending them because, now that you know why you have been starving yourself of success, you can finally see why knowing all of the how-to's in the world won't help you, if you don't give yourself permission to succeed.

After reading and applying the information in this book, I'll bet that you'll be able to use much of that self-help literature that didn't quite help you before, because now you can use the tools given here to give yourself permission to succeed. Let me remind you that much of the how-to-succeed information that's out there tends to be hard-hitting and bottom-line oriented, and focused upon how to get what you want—because that's precisely what it's designed to do.

A list of traditional self-help resources follows in For Further Learning.

The Success Clinic Programs/Success Counseling

The Success Clinic is the first and only center of its kind of which I am aware. To my knowledge, we offer the only programs in the world whose sole purpose is to work with people who want to stop starving themselves of success.

Success Counseling, the system I developed to help people overcome success anorexia, shows you how to stop starving yourself of the success you deserve, and enjoy all the personal and professional success that Life wants you to have.

I am currently developing a teaching program to bring Success Counseling to people around the world via global communication technology.

Please see the back of this book for more information on Success Counseling and other Success Clinic products and services.

EPILOGUE: THE LAST WORD ON SUCCESS

"He has achieved success who
has lived well, laughed often and loved
much; who has gained the respect of
intelligent people and the love of little
children; who has filled his niche and
accomplished his task; who has left the
world better than he found it, whether
by an improved poppy, a perfect poem
or a rescued soul; who has never lacked
appreciation of Earth's Beauty or failed
to express it; who has looked for the best
in others and given the best he had;
whose life was an inspiration;
whose memory is a benediction."

— MRS. A. J. STANLEY

"*To laugh often and much;*
To win the respect of intelligent people and the
affection of children;
To earn the appreciation of honest critics and
endure the betrayal of false friends;
To appreciate beauty;
To find the best in others;
To leave the world a little better, whether by a
healthy child, a garden
patch, or a redeemed social condition;
To know that even one life has breathed easier
because you have lived.
This is to have succeeded."

—RALPH WALDO EMERSON
(PARAPHRASING THE ABOVE POEM BY
MRS. A. J. STANLEY, ONE OF HIS CONTEMPORARIES)

FOR FURTHER LEARNING

The following resources have helped me to ask better questions in my life. I invite the reader to discover the wisdom they reveal. (This is by no means a comprehensive list.)

Books

Branden, Nathaniel. *The Six Pillars of Self-Esteem*. New York: Bantam, 1995.

Canfield, Jack and Mark Victor Hansen. *The Aladdin Factor*. New York: Berkley, 1995.

Carnegie, Dale. *How to Stop Worrying and Start Living*. New York: Simon & Schuster, 1944.

_____. *How to Win Friends and Influence People*. New York: Simon & Schuster, 1936.

Chopra, Deepak. *Perfect Health*. New York: Harmony Books, 1991.

Claude-Pierre, Peggy. *The Secret Language of Eating Disorders*. New York: Random House, 1997.

Covey, Stephen. *The 7 Habits of Highly Effective People*. New York: Simon & Schuster, 1989.

De Becker, Gavin. *The Gift of Fear*. New York: Little, Brown and Co., 1997.

Doniger O'Flaherty, Wendy. *Hindu Myths: A Sourcebook*. New York: Viking Press, 1975.

Frankl, Viktor. *Man's Search For Meaning*. 3rd ed. New York: Simon & Schuster, 1985.

_____. *The Will to Meaning*. New York: Simon & Schuster, 1989.

Hill, Napoleon. *Think and Grow Rich*. New York: Random House, 1937.

Holmes, Ernest. *The Science of Mind*. New York: G. P. Putnam's Sons, 1938.

_____. *Living The Science of Mind*. Marina del Rey, Calif.: DeVorss & Co., 1984.

Olivelle, Patrick. *The Upanisads: A New Translation*. New York: Oxford University Press, 1996.

Pilzer, Paul Zane. *God Wants You to Be Rich*. New York: Simon & Schuster, 1937.

Ponder, Catherine. *The Dynamic Laws of Prosperity*. Marina del Rey, Calif.: DeVorss & Co., 1985.

_____. *Open Your Mind to Receive*. Marina del Rey, Calif.: DeVorss & Co., 1983.

Riley, Pat. *The Winner Within*. New York: G. P. Putnam's Sons, 1993.

SARK. *Succulent Wild Woman*. New York: Fireside Books, 1997.

von Oech, Roger. *A Whack on the Side of the Head*. Rev. ed. New York: Warner Books, 1998.

Walsch, Neale Donald. *Conversations with God* (Books One, Two and Three). Hampton Roads, Va.: Hampton Roads, 1995–1998.

Audiotape Programs

Abraham, Jay. *Your Secret Wealth*. Niles, Ill.: Nightingale–Conant, 1994.

Covey, Stephen. *The 7 Habits of Highly Effective People*. Salt Lake City: Covey Leadership Center, 1997.

Dawson, Roger. *The Confident Decision Maker*. New York: Simon & Schuster (Audio), 1993.

Hill, Napoleon. *Think and Grow Rich*. Northbrook, Ill.: Napoleon Hill Foundation, 1987.

Robbins, Anthony. *Unlimited Power*. New York: Simon & Schuster (Audio), 1986.

WHO IS NOAH ST. JOHN?

Noah St. John leads The Success Clinic in Hadley, Massachusetts. He works with people who want to stop impeding their own success and with companies and organizations who want a happy, more productive work force.

In addition to working one-on-one, Noah conducts workshops and presentations designed to promote maximum growth using proven strategies for success. He works with team leaders and decision makers who want to maximize their return on their time, money and talent.

Noah emphasizes the importance of using correct principles to build a solid foundation for continual growth and long-term success, rather than quick-fix approaches that usually don't last.

Noah is the author of *Permission To Succeed* and publishes an electronic newsletter that is read by business owners and sales professionals in more than twenty-four countries around the world. He is currently working on the second and third books in this series, on how and why to let yourself succeed.

Noah has been profiled on numerous television, radio, online and print media, including Net Profits Radio, Success Weekly, Getting Personal with Linda Stein, People Are Talking, TalkBiz News, The Breakfast Club, RealVoices.com, The Book Authority, and ABC and NBC News.

For booking information and availability, contact:

The Success Clinic
P.O. Box 2773
Amherst, MA 01002
or visit us online at:
www.SuccessClinic.com

A New Season of
Chicken Soup for the Soul

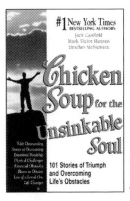

Chicken Soup for the Single Soul
Code #7060 • $12.95

Chicken Soup for the Unsinkable Soul
Code #6986 • $12.95

Chicken Soup for the Cat and Dog Lovers Soul
Code #7109 • $12.95

Chicken Soup for the College Soul
Code #7028 • $12.95

Each one of these new heartwarming titles will bring inspiration both to you and the loved ones in your life.

Transforming Anxiety, Transcending Shame

Rex Briggs, M.S.W.

If you suffer from anxiety, this groundbreaking book will provide a foundation for understanding the core causes of "excessive anxiety" and help you build specific, practical strategies for change.

Code #7222 Paperback • $11.95

This unique book interweaves the author's clinical expertise with his personal experience as a former anxiety sufferer and offers an incomparable blend of compassion and practical implementation that is sure to permanently transform your life. This book will teach you to understand the message your anxiety is sending you and how to respond to it.

The Heart of a Woman

A Memoir of Healing and Reversing Heart Disease

*A candid and intimate portrait, and a testament to the courage
and faith necessary to successfully undertake a journey of healing,
the magnitude of which inevitably results in self-transformation.*

Code #6935 Paperback • $10.95

This personal story of courage and perseverance from professional psychologist Pat Krantzler chronicles her enduring a
life-threatening heart attack, her physical and emotional
roller-coaster ride directly following the attack, her rehabilita-
tion, her ongoing efforts to reverse heart disease, and, above
all, her commitment to reclaiming her life and re-creating her
self-image.

Visionary Fiction from HCI

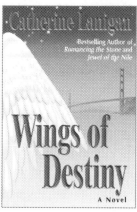

Wings of Destiny

Catherine Lanigan, best-selling author of *Romancing the Stone* and *Jewel of the Nile*, returns with a sweeping tale centered on the courage and irrepressible spirit of its protagonist heroine. The story of Jefferson Duke, who sacrifices the most precious of life's gifts: his heart and his granddaughter Barbara, who must betray him and, ultimately, learn the truth about herself and her own secret past.

Code #6900 Hardcover • $24.00

Rings of Truth

A profound tale of a man's journey to discover his true self. Matt, a motivational speaker, has it all, until a spiritual apparition allows him to see that his material success means nothing if his soul is empty. Follow him on his transformative journey of awareness and awakening as he develops a greater understanding of who he his and teaches those around him, one truth at a time.

Code #7249 Paperback • $12.95